Programming Across Platforms

Leveraging Python and C# to Create Dynamic, Responsive, and High-Performance Applications

THOMPSON CARTER

All rights reserved

Table of Content

TABLE OF CONTENTS

Introduction

Welcome to **"Programming Across Platforms: Leveraging Python and C# to Create Dynamic, Responsive, and High-Performance Applications."** Whether you're an experienced developer or just beginning your journey, this book is designed to guide you through the world of cross-platform development, focusing on two of the most powerful programming languages—**Python** and **C#**.

In today's fast-paced, interconnected world, building applications that work across multiple platforms is a necessity. As businesses and developers increasingly seek to reach users on a wide range of devices and operating systems—**Windows, macOS, Linux, mobile, and web**—the need for efficient cross-platform solutions has never been greater. This book aims to provide you with the tools and knowledge necessary to create versatile, dynamic applications using Python and C#, two languages that complement each other in the development ecosystem.

Why Cross-Platform Development?

Cross-platform development refers to the practice of writing code once and deploying it across different platforms—

without needing to rewrite the application for each platform. This approach allows developers to:

- **Save time** and **resources** by writing a single codebase that works across various environments.
- **Expand their reach** by ensuring their application runs on different operating systems, devices, and browsers.
- **Achieve consistency** in user experience and performance, regardless of the platform.

Building cross-platform applications also offers flexibility in choosing the most appropriate tools and technologies for specific needs, without being tied to a particular platform.

Why Python and C#?

While there are many programming languages available for cross-platform development, **Python** and **C#** stand out due to their versatility, performance, and broad adoption in the industry. This book focuses on how these two languages can work together (or individually) to create applications that are not only efficient but also highly scalable and maintainable.

- **Python**: Known for its simplicity and readability, Python is an excellent choice for scripting, web development, data science, machine learning, and automation. Its extensive ecosystem of libraries and frameworks—such as **Flask**, **Django**, **TensorFlow**, and **PyTorch**—make it a favorite for building everything from web apps to AI-powered systems.

- **C#**: A powerful, object-oriented language developed by **Microsoft**, C# excels in building **high-performance**, **enterprise-grade** applications. With frameworks like **ASP.NET**, **Xamarin**, and **.NET MAUI**, C# enables developers to create not only **desktop and mobile applications** but also **cloud-based solutions** and **games**.

By leveraging the strengths of both Python and C#, developers can build applications that are both **robust** and **highly performant** while remaining flexible enough to run on different platforms.

What This Book Offers

This book is structured to provide both theoretical knowledge and practical experience. You will learn how to:

1. **Set up your development environment** and get familiar with tools like **VS Code**, **PyCharm**, and **Visual Studio** for Python and C# development.

2. **Master the basics** of Python and C# syntax, libraries, and core concepts, ensuring that you're comfortable with both languages, regardless of your background.

3. **Build cross-platform applications** that can run seamlessly across Windows, macOS, and Linux. We'll cover various frameworks and deployment strategies to ensure that you can take full advantage of the strengths of each platform.

4. **Implement real-world solutions** to common development challenges. From working with databases and APIs to integrating machine learning models, you'll tackle problems that modern developers face.

5. **Optimize your code** for performance and scalability, focusing on **caching**, **memory management**, and **profiling** techniques to make sure your applications run smoothly even under heavy load.

6. **Understand cloud deployment** with strategies for hosting Python and C# applications on platforms like

AWS, **Azure**, and **Google Cloud**, along with implementing **serverless architectures**.

7. **Prepare for future trends** in cross-platform development, including the emerging technologies and frameworks such as **Flutter**, **.NET MAUI**, and **WebAssembly**, that will shape the future of app development.

The Real-World Approach

Each chapter of this book emphasizes **practical application**, with **real-world examples** to help you apply what you learn. These examples will guide you through the process of building useful applications, from basic concepts to advanced techniques. Whether it's building a simple **web API** or a **high-performance mobile app**, this book will provide you with step-by-step guidance to ensure you can successfully build and deploy cross-platform applications.

Who This Book is For

This book is perfect for developers who want to:

- **Expand their skillset** by mastering cross-platform development with Python and C#.

- **Develop full-stack applications** that run on multiple platforms, from desktop to web and mobile.

- **Learn best practices** for performance optimization, cloud deployment, and debugging, ensuring your applications are scalable and efficient.

- **Explore the intersection of machine learning, AI, and app development**, and learn how to integrate these technologies into real-world applications.

Whether you are a beginner eager to explore cross-platform development or an experienced developer looking to expand your expertise in Python and C#, this book will equip you with the knowledge and tools to build modern, powerful applications.

Next Steps

Throughout this book, you'll encounter **hands-on tutorials**, **code snippets**, and **practical challenges** to reinforce your learning. After completing this book, you will be equipped to:

- Build **dynamic, responsive, and high-performance applications** that work across multiple platforms.

- Leverage the power of **AI and machine learning** in your cross-platform apps.
- Implement **cloud solutions** and **serverless architectures** for scalable, cost-effective deployments.

With this knowledge, you'll be well-positioned to tackle modern development challenges, whether you're working on **enterprise software**, **consumer-facing apps**, or cutting-edge **AI-powered solutions**.

PART 1

FOUNDATIONS OF CROSS-PLATFORM PROGRAMMING

CHAPTER 1

INTRODUCTION TO CROSS-PLATFORM DEVELOPMENT

What is Cross-Platform Development?

In today's world, users access applications from various devices—laptops, smartphones, tablets, and even smart TVs. Cross-platform development is the practice of writing code that works across multiple operating systems without needing major modifications.

Instead of developing separate applications for **Windows, macOS, Linux, Web, and Mobile**, cross-platform development allows developers to **write once and deploy everywhere**. This not only saves time and effort but also ensures a **consistent user experience** across different devices.

Key Benefits of Cross-Platform Development

- **Cost-Efficient:** Write code once instead of maintaining separate codebases for different platforms.

- **Faster Development:** Avoid duplicating effort, reducing development time significantly.
- **Wider Reach:** Target a broader audience by making applications available on multiple platforms.
- **Easier Maintenance:** Bug fixes and updates are applied to one codebase, benefiting all platforms simultaneously.

Why Python and C#? Strengths and Weaknesses

Both Python and C# are powerful languages with unique advantages. Here's why they are ideal for cross-platform development:

Python: A Versatile, High-Level Language

Strengths:
Easy to learn and use, with a simple syntax
Supports multiple platforms out of the box
Rich ecosystem of libraries (e.g., Flask, Django, TensorFlow, Pandas)
Great for scripting, automation, web development, and AI

Weaknesses:
Slower than compiled languages like C#
Not ideal for building high-performance desktop

25

applications

Limited mobile development support (compared to C# with Xamarin)

C#: A Strongly Typed, High-Performance Language

Strengths:

Runs efficiently on Windows, macOS, and Linux with .NET Core

Excellent for enterprise applications, desktop apps, and game   development

Strong support for mobile development with Xamarin and MAUI

Ideal for building high-performance and scalable applications

Weaknesses:

Slightly steeper learning curve compared to Python

More verbose syntax, requiring more code for simple tasks

Primarily Microsoft-driven, though now more open-source

How Python and C# Complement Each Other

By leveraging **Python's simplicity and flexibility** along with **C#'s performance and scalability**, developers can build powerful cross-platform applications that balance speed, usability, and efficiency.

Overview of Platforms: Windows, macOS, Linux, Web, and Mobile

Windows:

- The most widely used desktop OS
- Strong support for .NET applications (C#)
- Can run Python with ease

macOS:

- Preferred by many developers
- Supports both Python and .NET Core (C#)
- Good environment for cross-platform development

Linux:

- The go-to choice for servers and cloud applications
- Python is natively supported
- .NET Core allows C# applications to run smoothly

Web Applications:

- Python (Flask, Django) and C# (ASP.NET Core) can build full-stack web apps
- Can be accessed across any device with a browser

Mobile Applications:

- **Python** supports mobile development through Kivy and BeeWare (less mature)
- **C#** shines with Xamarin and .NET MAUI, making it a better mobile choice

By choosing the right framework, developers can build **cross-platform applications that run seamlessly** on multiple devices.

Real-World Examples of Successful Cross-Platform Applications

Dropbox (Python):

- Initially built using Python
- Runs on Windows, macOS, Linux, iOS, and Android

Unity Game Engine (C#):

- Uses C# as its primary language
- Allows developers to create games for PC, consoles, mobile, and VR

Spotify (Python & C# Hybrid):

- Uses Python for backend services
- Uses C# for its Windows desktop client

Instagram (Python):

- Backend is powered by Python/Django
- Works across web and mobile platforms

Microsoft Teams (C#):

- Built using .NET and C#
- Works on Windows, macOS, and mobile

Conclusion

Cross-platform development is essential in today's software world. **Python and C# offer unique strengths that, when combined, allow developers to create fast, scalable, and user-friendly applications.**

In the next chapter, we'll set up our development environment, ensuring you have everything needed to start building cross-platform applications.

CHAPTER 2

SETTING UP YOUR DEVELOPMENT ENVIRONMENT

Before we dive into writing code, it's essential to set up a proper development environment. This chapter will guide you through installing **Python and C# (.NET Core)** on different operating systems, choosing the right **integrated development environment (IDE)**, managing **dependencies**, and using **version control with Git and GitHub**.

Installing Python and C# (.NET Core) on Different Operating Systems

Since we are working with **Python and C#** for cross-platform development, we need to install both on **Windows, macOS, and Linux**.

Installing Python

Python is available for all major operating systems.

Windows:

1. Go to the official Python website.
2. Download the latest **stable** version for Windows.
3. During installation, **check the box** that says **"Add Python to PATH"** (important!).
4. Verify installation by opening the command prompt (cmd) and running:

```css

python --version
```

macOS:

1. macOS comes with Python pre-installed, but it's usually outdated.
2. Install the latest version using **Homebrew** (if not installed, first install Homebrew using brew.sh):

```nginx

brew install python
```

3. Verify installation:

```css

python3 --version
```

Linux (Ubuntu/Debian-based):

1. Open the terminal and install Python:

```sql
```

```
sudo apt update
sudo apt install python3 python3-pip
```

2. Verify installation:

```css
```

```
python3 --version
```

Installing C# (.NET Core)

.NET Core allows C# applications to run across different platforms.

Windows:

1. Download the latest .NET SDK from Microsoft's official site.
2. Run the installer and follow the setup instructions.
3. Verify installation by opening PowerShell or Command Prompt and running:

33

```
css
```

```
dotnet --version
```

macOS:

1. Install .NET SDK using **Homebrew**:

```
nginx
```

```
brew install dotnet-sdk
```

2. Verify installation:

```
css
```

```
dotnet --version
```

Linux (Ubuntu/Debian-based):

1. Install required dependencies:

```
sql
```

```
sudo apt update && sudo apt install -y
dotnet-sdk-7.0
```

2. Verify installation:

```
css
```

```
dotnet --version
```

Setting Up IDEs: Choosing the Right Development Environment

An Integrated Development Environment (IDE) helps write, test, and debug code efficiently. The choice of IDE depends on preference and project requirements.

Best IDEs for Python and C# Development

IDE	Best for	Supported Languages	Pros
Visual Studio Code	Python & C#	Python, C#, JS, etc.	Lightweight, cross-platform, great extensions
PyCharm	Python	Python	Best Python experience, built-in debugging
Visual Studio	C#	C#, F#, C++	Best for .NET development, powerful debugging tools

IDE	Best for	Supported Languages	Pros
JetBrains Rider	C#	C#, .NET	Fast, smart code analysis, best for enterprise .NET

Installing Visual Studio Code (VS Code) (Recommended for Cross-Platform Development)

1. Download from VS Code website.
2. Install extensions for Python (Python) and C# (C# Dev Kit).

Installing PyCharm (For Python Development)

1. Download from JetBrains website.
2. Use the **Community Edition** (free) or **Professional Edition** (paid).

Installing Visual Studio (For C# Development)

1. Download from Visual Studio website.
2. Choose the **.NET Core cross-platform development** workload during installation.

Installing JetBrains Rider (For Advanced C# Development)

1. Download from JetBrains website.
2. Requires a **JetBrains account** (offers a free trial).

Managing Dependencies with pip, NuGet, and Package Managers

Most applications rely on external libraries to extend functionality. Managing these dependencies properly is crucial.

Managing Dependencies in Python with `pip`

Checking if pip is installed:

css

```
pip --version
```

Installing a package (e.g., Flask):

nginx

```
pip install flask
```

Listing installed packages:

nginx

37

```
pip list
```

Creating a `requirements.txt` file for project dependencies:

```
pgsql
```

```
pip freeze > requirements.txt
```

Installing dependencies from `requirements.txt`:

```
nginx
```

```
pip install -r requirements.txt
```

Managing Dependencies in C# with NuGet

NuGet is the package manager for .NET applications.

Installing a package (e.g., Newtonsoft.Json):

```
pgsql
```

```
dotnet add package Newtonsoft.Json
```

Listing installed packages:

```
go
```

```
dotnet list package
```

Restoring dependencies from a project file:

```
nginx
```

```
dotnet restore
```

Both **pip (Python)** and **NuGet (C#)** ensure your projects have the correct dependencies for seamless cross-platform functionality.

Version Control with Git and GitHub

Version control is essential for tracking changes and collaborating on projects. Git and GitHub make it easy to manage and share code.

Installing Git

Windows: Install Git from git-scm.com.
macOS: Install via Homebrew:

```
nginx
```

```
brew install git
```

39

Linux: Install via package manager:

```
nginx
```

```
sudo apt install git
```

Basic Git Commands

Configuring Git for the first time:

```
arduino
```

```
git config --global user.name "Your Name"
git config --global user.email
"youremail@example.com"
```

Cloning a GitHub repository:

```
bash
```

```
git                                    clone
https://github.com/username/repository.git
```

Adding and committing changes:

```
sql
```

```
git add .
git commit -m "Initial commit"
```

Pushing code to GitHub:

css

```
git push origin main
```

Pulling updates from a remote repository:

css

```
git pull origin main
```

Creating a New GitHub Repository

1. Go to GitHub.
2. Click on **New Repository**.
3. Give it a name and select **Initialize with a README**.
4. the remote URL and run:

    csharp

    ```
    git remote add origin <repo_url>
    git push -u origin main
    ```

Using **Git and GitHub** ensures you never lose code and makes collaboration easy, especially for large cross-platform projects.

Conclusion

Setting up a proper development environment is the first step in building efficient cross-platform applications. In this chapter, we covered:
Installing **Python and C# (.NET Core)** on Windows, macOS, and Linux
Choosing the right **IDE** for Python and C# development
Managing **dependencies** with `pip` (Python) and `NuGet` (C#)
Using **Git and GitHub** for version control

With everything set up, you are now ready to start writing cross-platform applications. In the next chapter, we'll **compare Python and C# syntax** to help you understand the differences and similarities.

CHAPTER 3

PROGRAMMING BASICS – PYTHON VS. C#

Python and C# are both powerful programming languages, but they have different syntax, structures, and philosophies.

Understanding the **differences and similarities** between them will help you develop cross-platform applications efficiently.

---

1. Syntax Comparison of Python and C#

Python is **dynamically typed** and **interpreted**, meaning you don't need to declare variable types explicitly. C# is **statically typed** and **compiled**, requiring type declarations.

Basic "Hello, World!" in Python and C#

Python (Simple and Concise)

```python
print("Hello, World!")
```

C# (More Structured and Explicit)

```csharp
using System;

class Program {
    static void Main() {
        Console.WriteLine("Hello, World!");
```

43

```
    }
}
```

Key Differences:

- **Python is more concise** – no need for a `Main()` method.
- **C# enforces structure** with a class and method.
- **Python uses indentation**, while **C# uses curly braces** `{}`.

---

2. Data Types, Variables, and Operators

Declaring Variables in Python vs. C#

Python (Dynamic Typing, No Need to Specify Types)

```python
python
```

```python
name = "Alice"
age = 25
price = 19.99
is_valid = True
```

C# (Static Typing, Requires Type Declaration)

```csharp
csharp
```

```csharp
string name = "Alice";
```

44

```
int age = 25;
double price = 19.99;
bool isValid = true;
```

Key Differences:

- **Python infers types dynamically**, while **C# requires explicit type declarations**.
- C# uses **semicolon (;)** at the end of each statement.

Common Data Types

Data Type	Python Example	C# Example
String	name = "Alice"	string name = "Alice";
Integer	age = 30	int age = 30;
Float	price = 9.99	double price = 9.99;
Boolean	is_valid = True	bool isValid = true;
List/Array	numbers = [1, 2, 3]	int[] numbers = {1, 2, 3};

Operators in Python vs. C#

Operator	Python Example	C# Example
Addition	`x = 5 + 2`	`int x = 5 + 2;`
Subtraction	`y = 10 - 3`	`int y = 10 - 3;`
Multiplication	`z = 4 * 3`	`int z = 4 * 3;`
Division	`a = 10 / 3`	`double a = 10.0 / 3;`
Modulus	`b = 10 % 3`	`int b = 10 % 3;`
Power	`c = 2 ** 3`	`double c = Math.Pow(2, 3);`
Logical AND	`x and y`	`x && y`
Logical OR	`x or y`	`` `x ``

3. Control Structures: Loops, Conditionals, and Functions

Conditionals (`if-else`)

Python (No parentheses, uses indentation)

```python
```

```
age = 18

if age >= 18:
    print("You are an adult.")
else:
    print("You are a minor.")
```

C# (Uses curly braces and parentheses)

```
csharp

int age = 18;

if (age >= 18) {
    Console.WriteLine("You are an adult.");
} else {
    Console.WriteLine("You are a minor.");
}
```

Key Differences:

- Python **uses indentation**, while C# **uses { } brackets**.
- C# **requires parentheses** around conditions.

Loops (`for` and `while`)

Python `for` loop (iterates directly over elements)

```python
python
```

```python
for i in range(5):
    print(i)
```

C# `for` loop (uses an index-based approach)

```csharp
csharp
```

```csharp
for (int i = 0; i < 5; i++) {
    Console.WriteLine(i);
}
```

Python `while` loop

```python
python
```

```python
x = 0
while x < 5:
    print(x)
    x += 1
```

C# `while` loop

```csharp
csharp
```

```csharp
int x = 0;
while (x < 5) {
    Console.WriteLine(x);
    x++;
```

```
}
```

Key Differences:

- Python's `for` loop iterates over a sequence, while C#'s `for` loop uses an **index-based structure**.
- Both languages have `while` loops with a **similar syntax**.

4. Object-Oriented Programming (OOP) in Python and C#

Both **Python and C# are object-oriented**, but their implementation differs.

Defining a Class and Creating an Object

Python (Simpler, No Explicit Types)

```python
python

class Person:
    def __init__(self, name, age):
        self.name = name
        self.age = age

    def greet(self):
        return f"Hello, my name is {self.name}."
```

49

```
person1 = Person("Alice", 25)
print(person1.greet())
```

C# (More Structured, Requires Types)

```csharp
using System;

class Person {
    public string Name;
    public int Age;

    public Person(string name, int age) {
        Name = name;
        Age = age;
    }

    public string Greet() {
        return $"Hello, my name is {Name}.";
    }
}

class Program {
    static void Main() {
        Person person1 = new Person("Alice", 25);
        Console.WriteLine(person1.Greet());
    }
}
```

Key Differences:

- **Python does not require explicit types**, while **C#** **enforces type safety**.
- **Python uses `self` instead of `this`** for referring to class attributes.
- **C# requires `Main()` method** for program execution.

Conclusion

This chapter covered the fundamental differences between Python and C#, focusing on:
Syntax comparison
Data types, variables, and operators
Control structures (loops, conditionals, functions)
Object-Oriented Programming (OOP)

In the next chapter, we'll explore **Cross-Platform Design Principles**, discussing best practices for writing code that runs efficiently across **Windows, macOS, Linux, and mobile devices**.

CHAPTER 4

CROSS-PLATFORM DESIGN PRINCIPLES

Building **cross-platform applications** requires more than just choosing the right programming language. It's about writing **efficient, reusable, and maintainable code** while handling platform-specific differences. This chapter explores the key principles that ensure smooth operation across **Windows, macOS, Linux, Web, and Mobile**.

---

1. Writing Reusable and Maintainable Code

Cross-platform development benefits from **reusability**—writing code that works across multiple platforms without modification. But reusable code should also be **maintainable**, meaning it is **easy to read, update, and debug**.

Key Strategies for Reusable Code

Follow the DRY Principle (Don't Repeat Yourself)

52

- Avoid duplicating code by using **functions, classes, and modules**.
- Example in Python:

```python
def greet(name):
    return f"Hello, {name}!"


print(greet("Alice"))
print(greet("Bob"))
```

Example in C#:

```csharp
class Program {
    static string Greet(string name) {
        return $"Hello, {name}!";
    }

    static void Main() {

Console.WriteLine(Greet("Alice"));
        Console.WriteLine(Greet("Bob"));
    }
}
```

Use Modular Architecture

- Break applications into **smaller components** (e.g., modules, services, APIs).
- This allows different parts of the code to be **reused independently**.
- Example: Separating database logic from business logic.

Follow Consistent Naming Conventions

- **Python:** Use `snake_case` for variables and functions.
- **C#:** Use `PascalCase` for classes and `camelCase` for variables.

Document Code Clearly

- Use comments and **docstrings** (Python) or **XML documentation** (C#).
- Example in Python:

```python
def add_numbers(a, b):
    """Returns the sum of two numbers."""
    return a + b
```

- Example in C#:

```csharp
/// <summary>
```

54

```
/// Adds two numbers and returns the
result.
/// </summary>
static int AddNumbers(int a, int b) {
    return a + b;
}
```

2. Handling Platform-Specific Differences

Even though Python and C# allow cross-platform development, some **system-level differences** must be handled carefully.

File System Differences

Windows: Uses backslashes (C:\Users\Alice)
Linux/macOS: Uses forward slashes (/home/alice)

Solution: Use OS-Agnostic Paths
Python Example:

```python
import os

file_path = os.path.join("home", "user", "data.txt")  # Works on all OS
```

C# Example:

```
csharp

using System.IO;

string filePath = Path.Combine("home", "user",
"data.txt");  // Works on all OS
```

Line Ending Differences (CRLF vs. LF)

- **Windows:** Uses \r\n (CRLF) for new lines.
- **Linux/macOS:** Uses \n (LF) for new lines.

Solution: Normalize   Line   Endings
Python Example:

```python
python

text = "Hello, World!\n"   # Use \n to ensure
consistency
```

C# Example:

```
csharp

string    text    =    "Hello,    World!"    +
Environment.NewLine;
```

System Commands and OS Interactions

- **Windows:** Uses `dir`, `cls` (Command Prompt).
- **Linux/macOS:** Uses `ls`, `clear` (Bash).

Solution: Use `platform` Module in Python

```python
python

import os, platform

if platform.system() == "Windows":
    os.system("cls")
else:
    os.system("clear")
```

Solution: Use `RuntimeInformation` in C#

```csharp
csharp

using System;
using System.Runtime.InteropServices;

if
(RuntimeInformation.IsOSPlatform(OSPlatform.Win
dows)) {
    Console.WriteLine("Running on Windows");
```

57

```
} else {
    Console.WriteLine("Running on Linux/macOS");
}
```

3. Using Abstraction Layers to Minimize Platform
Dependencies

An **abstraction layer** helps **decouple** platform-specific
logic from the main application, making it easier to adapt to
different operating systems.

Example: Using Interfaces to Abstract File Operations in C#

csharp

```
public interface IFileHandler {
    void Save(string content);
}

public class WindowsFileHandler : IFileHandler {
    public void Save(string content) {
        File.WriteAllText("C:\\data.txt",
content);
    }
}
```

```
public class LinuxFileHandler : IFileHandler {
    public void Save(string content) {

File.WriteAllText("/home/user/data.txt",
content);
    }
}
```

The **main application** can choose the correct file handler at runtime based on the OS.

Example: Using Functions to Abstract System Calls in Python

```python
import os, platform

def clear_screen():
    if platform.system() == "Windows":
        os.system("cls")
    else:
        os.system("clear")

clear_screen()
```

This approach keeps the **main code clean** and reduces platform-specific modifications.

4. Performance Considerations for Cross-Platform Apps

Cross-platform applications must be **efficient** to avoid performance issues.

Optimizing Python Code

Use Built-in Functions Instead of Loops

python

```
# Slow approach
squared = []
for num in range(10):
    squared.append(num ** 2)


# Faster approach using list comprehension
squared = [num ** 2 for num in range(10)]
```

Use Generators for Large Data Processing

python

```
def generate_numbers():
    for i in range(1_000_000):
        yield i  # Does not store all numbers in
memory
```

60

```
for num in generate_numbers():
    print(num)
```

Optimizing C# Code

Use StringBuilder for String Concatenation

csharp

```
using System.Text;

StringBuilder sb = new StringBuilder();
sb.Append("Hello ");
sb.Append("World!");
Console.WriteLine(sb.ToString());
```

Why? StringBuilder is more efficient than + for repeated string concatenation.

Use Asynchronous Programming to Avoid Blocking Operations

csharp

```
using System;
using System.Threading.Tasks;
```

```
class Program {
    static async Task Main() {
        await           Task.Run(()              =>
Console.WriteLine("Processing..."));
    }
}
```

Why? Asynchronous programming **prevents blocking** the main thread.

Conclusion

By following cross-platform **design principles**, you can write applications that work seamlessly across **Windows, macOS, Linux, Web, and Mobile**.

Write reusable and maintainable code Handle platform-specific differences Use abstraction layers to separate platform logic Optimize performance to avoid inefficiencies

In the next chapter, we'll **build our first console applications in Python and C#** to apply these principles in practice.

PART 2
CORE APPLICATION DEVELOPMENT

CHAPTER 5

BUILDING CONSOLE APPLICATIONS

Console applications are **lightweight, fast, and cross-platform**, making them ideal for automation, system utilities, and backend services. This chapter will cover how to **build command-line tools** in **Python and C#**, handle **user input/output**, work with **files and directories**, and create a **real-world task manager**.

1. Creating Command-Line Tools with Python and C#

Command-line tools allow users to **interact with applications via text commands** instead of a graphical interface.

Creating a Simple CLI in Python

```python
import sys
```

```
def main():
    if len(sys.argv) < 2:
        print("Usage: python app.py <name>")
        sys.exit(1)

    name = sys.argv[1]
    print(f"Hello, {name}!")

if __name__ == "__main__":
    main()
```

How it works:

- Uses `sys.argv` to accept command-line arguments.
- Runs with:

```
nginx
```

```
python app.py Alice
```

- Output:

```
Hello, Alice!
```

Creating a Simple CLI in C#

```
csharp
```

```
using System;

class Program {
    static void Main(string[] args) {
        if (args.Length < 1) {
            Console.WriteLine("Usage: dotnet run
<name>");
            return;
        }

        string name = args[0];
        Console.WriteLine($"Hello, {name}!");
    }
}
```

How it works:

- Uses `args[]` to accept user input from the command line.
- Runs with:

```
arduino
```

```
dotnet run Alice
```

- Output:

```
Hello, Alice!
```

2. Handling User Input and Output

Console applications **communicate with users** through standard input (`stdin`) and output (`stdout`).

Python: Getting User Input and Printing Output

```python
python
```

```python
name = input("Enter your name: ")
print(f"Hello, {name}!")
```

Example Run:

```yaml
yaml
```

```
Enter your name: Alice
Hello, Alice!
```

C#: Getting User Input and Printing Output

```csharp
csharp
```

```csharp
using System;

class Program {
    static void Main() {
        Console.Write("Enter your name: ");
        string name = Console.ReadLine();
```

```
        Console.WriteLine($"Hello, {name}!");
    }
}
```

Example Run:

```
yaml


Enter your name: Alice
Hello, Alice!
```

---

3. Working with Files and Directories

Console applications often read and write files for **data storage**.

Python: Reading and Writing Files

```python
# Writing to a file
with open("data.txt", "w") as file:
    file.write("Hello, World!\n")

# Reading from a file
with open("data.txt", "r") as file:
    content = file.read()
    print(content)
```

C#: Reading and Writing Files

```csharp
using System;
using System.IO;

class Program {
    static void Main() {
        string path = "data.txt";

        // Writing to a file
        File.WriteAllText(path,          "Hello,
World!\n");

        // Reading from a file
        string content = File.ReadAllText(path);
        Console.WriteLine(content);
    }
}
```

Key Differences:

- **Python uses with open()** to handle files safely.
- **C#   uses   `File.WriteAllText()`   and** `File.ReadAllText()` for quick file operations.

4. Real-World Example: A Simple Task Manager

Now, let's create a **Task Manager CLI** that allows users to **add, list, and remove tasks**.

Python: Task Manager CLI

```python
import os

TASKS_FILE = "tasks.txt"

def load_tasks():
    if not os.path.exists(TASKS_FILE):
        return []
    with open(TASKS_FILE, "r") as file:
        return file.read().splitlines()

def save_tasks(tasks):
    with open(TASKS_FILE, "w") as file:
        file.write("\n".join(tasks))

def add_task(task):
    tasks = load_tasks()
    tasks.append(task)
    save_tasks(tasks)
```

70

```python
    print(f"Task added: {task}")


def list_tasks():
    tasks = load_tasks()
    if not tasks:
        print("No tasks found.")
    else:
        for i, task in enumerate(tasks, 1):
            print(f"{i}. {task}")


def remove_task(task_number):
    tasks = load_tasks()
    if 0 < task_number <= len(tasks):
        removed = tasks.pop(task_number - 1)
        save_tasks(tasks)
        print(f"Task removed: {removed}")
    else:
        print("Invalid task number.")


def main():
    while True:
        command = input("Enter command
(add/list/remove/exit): ").strip().lower()
        if command == "add":
            task = input("Enter task: ").strip()
            add_task(task)
        elif command == "list":
            list_tasks()
        elif command == "remove":
```

71

```
        list_tasks()
        task_number = int(input("Enter task
number to remove: "))
        remove_task(task_number)
    elif command == "exit":
        print("Goodbye!")
        break
    else:
        print("Invalid command.")

if __name__ == "__main__":
    main()
```

How it works:

- Tasks are stored in `tasks.txt`.
- **Commands:** `add`, `list`, `remove`, `exit`.
- Runs with:

```
nginx
```

```
python task_manager.py
```

C#: Task Manager CLI

```
csharp
```

```
using System;
```

```csharp
using System.Collections.Generic;
using System.IO;

class TaskManager {
    static string filePath = "tasks.txt";

    static List<string> LoadTasks() {
        return File.Exists(filePath) ? new
List<string>(File.ReadAllLines(filePath)) : new
List<string>();
    }

    static void SaveTasks(List<string> tasks) {
        File.WriteAllLines(filePath, tasks);
    }

    static void AddTask(string task) {
        List<string> tasks = LoadTasks();
        tasks.Add(task);
        SaveTasks(tasks);
        Console.WriteLine($"Task          added:
{task}");
    }

    static void ListTasks() {
        List<string> tasks = LoadTasks();
        if (tasks.Count == 0) {
            Console.WriteLine("No          tasks
found.");
```

```
        } else {
            for (int i = 0; i < tasks.Count; i++)
{
                Console.WriteLine($"{i   +   1}.
{tasks[i]}");
            }
        }
    }

    static void RemoveTask(int taskNumber) {
        List<string> tasks = LoadTasks();
        if (taskNumber > 0 && taskNumber <=
tasks.Count) {
            string removed = tasks[taskNumber -
1];
            tasks.RemoveAt(taskNumber - 1);
            SaveTasks(tasks);
            Console.WriteLine($"Task    removed:
{removed}");
        } else {
            Console.WriteLine("Invalid     task
number.");
        }
    }

    static void Main() {
        while (true) {
            Console.Write("Enter        command
(add/list/remove/exit): ");
```

74

```
        string         command         =
Console.ReadLine().Trim().ToLower();

        if (command == "add") {
            Console.Write("Enter task: ");
            string         task         =
Console.ReadLine().Trim();
            AddTask(task);
        } else if (command == "list") {
            ListTasks();
        } else if (command == "remove") {
            ListTasks();
            Console.Write("Enter task number
to remove: ");
            int         taskNumber         =
int.Parse(Console.ReadLine());
            RemoveTask(taskNumber);
        } else if (command == "exit") {
            Console.WriteLine("Goodbye!");
            break;
        } else {
            Console.WriteLine("Invalid
command.");
        }
    }
    }
  }
}
```

How it works:

75

- Tasks are stored in `tasks.txt`.
- **Commands:** `add`, `list`, `remove`, `exit`.
- Runs with:

```
arduino
```

```
dotnet run
```

Conclusion

In this chapter, we covered: **Creating console applications** in Python and C# **Handling user input and output** **Reading and writing files** **Building a task manager**

Next, we will explore **"Working with APIs and Web Services"** to connect applications to external data sources.

CHAPTER 6

WORKING WITH APIS AND WEB SERVICES

APIs (Application Programming Interfaces) allow applications to communicate with each other. In this chapter, we'll learn how to:
Call RESTful APIs using Python (`requests`) and C# (`HttpClient`)
Build a simple API with Flask (Python) and ASP.NET Core (C#)
Handle authentication and API responses
Fetch and display weather data from an API

---

1. Calling RESTful APIs Using Python (`requests`) and C# (`HttpClient`)

Making an API Request in Python (`requests`)

The `requests` module is used to fetch data from APIs in Python.

Example: Fetching Data from a Public API (JSON Placeholder)

```python
python

import requests

url                                    =
"https://jsonplaceholder.typicode.com/todos/1"
response = requests.get(url)

if response.status_code == 200:
    data = response.json()  # Convert response to
dictionary
    print(f"Task: {data['title']}")
else:
    print("Failed to retrieve data")
```

Output:

```arduino
arduino

Task: delectus aut autem
```

Key Concepts:

- `requests.get(url)` fetches data from an API.
- `.json()` converts JSON response to a Python dictionary.

- `response.status_code` helps check if the request was successful (`200 OK`).

Making an API Request in C# (`HttpClient`)

C# uses the `HttpClient` class to call APIs.

Example: Fetching Data from a Public API (JSON Placeholder)

csharp

```csharp
using System;
using System.Net.Http;
using System.Threading.Tasks;
using Newtonsoft.Json.Linq;

class Program {
    static async Task Main() {
        HttpClient client = new HttpClient();
        string                url                =
"https://jsonplaceholder.typicode.com/todos/1";

        HttpResponseMessage response = await
client.GetAsync(url);
        if (response.IsSuccessStatusCode) {
```

```
            string       json       =       await
response.Content.ReadAsStringAsync();
          var data = JObject.Parse(json);
          Console.WriteLine($"Task:
{data["title"]}");
       } else {
          Console.WriteLine("Failed          to
retrieve data");
       }
    }
}
```

Output:

```
arduino
```

```
Task: delectus aut autem
```

Key Concepts:

- `HttpClient.GetAsync(url)` **fetches API data.**
- `response.Content.ReadAsStringAsync()` converts response to a string.
- `JObject.Parse(json)` (from `Newtonsoft.Json`) parses JSON data.

2. Building a Simple API with Flask (Python) and ASP.NET Core (C#)

Creating a REST API with Flask (Python)

Flask makes it easy to build APIs.

Install Flask:

```sh
sh
```

```sh
pip install flask
```

Flask API Code (save as `app.py`)

```python
python
```

```python
from flask import Flask, jsonify

app = Flask(__name__)

@app.route("/api/greet/<name>")
def greet(name):
    return     jsonify({"message":     f"Hello, {name}!"})

if __name__ == "__main__":
    app.run(debug=True)
```

Run the API:

```sh
```

```
python app.py
```

Test the API in a browser:

```ruby
```

```
http://127.0.0.1:5000/api/greet/Alice
```

Response:

```json
```

```
{"message": "Hello, Alice!"}
```

Creating a REST API with ASP.NET Core (C#)

ASP.NET Core is used for scalable, high-performance APIs.

Create a New API Project:

```sh
```

```
dotnet new webapi -n MyApi
cd MyApi
dotnet run
```

Modify `Controllers/WeatherForecastController.cs` to Add a Greeting API:

csharp

```csharp
using Microsoft.AspNetCore.Mvc;

[ApiController]
[Route("api")]
public class GreetingController : ControllerBase
{
    [HttpGet("greet/{name}")]
    public IActionResult Greet(string name) {
        return Ok(new { message = $"Hello, {name}!" });
    }
}
```

Run the API:

sh

```sh
dotnet run
```

Test the API in a browser:

bash

```bash
http://localhost:5000/api/greet/Alice
```

Response:

```json
json
```

```json
{"message": "Hello, Alice!"}
```

3. Authentication and Handling API Responses

Some APIs require **authentication** via **API keys, OAuth, or tokens**.

Using API Keys in Python (`requests`)

```python
python

import requests

API_KEY = "your_api_key"
url                                    =
f"https://api.example.com/data?api_key={API_KEY
}"

response = requests.get(url)
if response.status_code == 200:
    print(response.json())
else:
    print("Authentication failed")
```

Using API Keys in C# (`HttpClient`)

csharp

```csharp
using System.Net.Http;
using System.Threading.Tasks;

class Program {
    static async Task Main() {
        HttpClient client = new HttpClient();
        string apiKey = "your_api_key";
        string url = $"https://api.example.com/data?api_key={apiKey}";


client.DefaultRequestHeaders.Add("Authorization", $"Bearer {apiKey}");
        HttpResponseMessage response = await client.GetAsync(url);

        if (response.IsSuccessStatusCode) {
            string json = await response.Content.ReadAsStringAsync();
            Console.WriteLine(json);
        } else {
            Console.WriteLine("Authentication failed");
        }
```

```
    }
}
```

Best Practices:

- **Never hardcode API keys** in the source code.
- **Use environment variables** or configuration files to store API keys securely.

---

4. Real-World Example: Fetching and Displaying Weather Data

Fetching Weather Data in Python (`requests`)

```python
python

import requests

API_KEY = "your_api_key"
city = "London"
url                                 =
f"http://api.weatherapi.com/v1/current.json?key
={API_KEY}&q={city}"

response = requests.get(url)
if response.status_code == 200:
    data = response.json()
```

```python
    print(f"Weather          in          {city}:
{data['current']['temp_c']}°C")
else:
    print("Failed to fetch weather data")
```

Example Output:

```
yaml


Weather in London: 15°C
```

Fetching Weather Data in C# (`HttpClient`)

```csharp
csharp


using System;
using System.Net.Http;
using System.Threading.Tasks;
using Newtonsoft.Json.Linq;

class Program {
    static async Task Main() {
        string apiKey = "your_api_key";
        string city = "London";
        string          url          =
$"http://api.weatherapi.com/v1/current.json?key
={apiKey}&q={city}";
```

```
       HttpClient client = new HttpClient();
       HttpResponseMessage response = await
client.GetAsync(url);

       if (response.IsSuccessStatusCode) {
           string       json       =       await
response.Content.ReadAsStringAsync();
           var data = JObject.Parse(json);
           Console.WriteLine($"Weather          in
{city}: {data["current"]["temp_c"]}°C");
       } else {
           Console.WriteLine("Failed to fetch
weather data");
       }
    }
}
```

Example Output:

yaml

Weather in London: 15°C

Conclusion

In   this   chapter,   we   covered:

Calling APIs using requests (Python) and HttpClient (C#)

Building APIs with Flask (Python) and ASP.NET Core (C#)

Handling authentication and API responses

Fetching and displaying real-world weather data

In the next chapter, we will explore **"Database Integration: SQL & NoSQL"**, where we'll connect Python and C# applications to databases like SQLite, PostgreSQL, and MongoDB.

CHAPTER 7

DATABASE INTEGRATION – SQL & NOSQL

Databases are essential for storing, retrieving, and managing data in applications. This chapter explores: **SQL & NoSQL databases** (SQLite, PostgreSQL, MongoDB)

Connecting to databases in **Python (`sqlite3`, `SQLAlchemy`)** and **C# (`Entity Framework Core`)**

Building a real-world multi-user notes application

---

1. Working with SQL & NoSQL Databases

SQL vs. NoSQL – What's the Difference?

Feature	SQL (Relational)	NoSQL (Non-Relational)
Structure	Tables with rows & columns	Documents, key-value, graphs
Schema	Strictly defined	Flexible, dynamic

Feature	SQL (Relational)	NoSQL (Non-Relational)
Scaling	Vertical scaling (strong consistency)	Horizontal scaling (better for large data)
Examples	SQLite, PostgreSQL, MySQL	MongoDB, Firebase, Cassandra

SQL (Relational): Good for structured data, banking systems, e-commerce.

NoSQL (Non-Relational): Best for dynamic, scalable apps like social media, analytics.

---

2. Connecting to Databases Using Python (sqlite3, SQLAlchemy)

Using SQLite (Lightweight SQL Database)

SQLite is an embedded, file-based database, perfect for small projects.

Installing SQLite:

```sh
sh
```

```
pip install sqlite3
```

Python: Connecting to SQLite and Creating a Table

```
python
```

```python
import sqlite3

conn = sqlite3.connect("notes.db")    # Create
database file
cursor = conn.cursor()

# Create a table
cursor.execute("""
CREATE TABLE IF NOT EXISTS notes (
    id INTEGER PRIMARY KEY AUTOINCREMENT,
    user TEXT NOT NULL,
    note TEXT NOT NULL
)
""")

conn.commit()
conn.close()
```

Inserting Data into SQLite

```
python
```

```python
conn = sqlite3.connect("notes.db")
cursor = conn.cursor()
```

92

```
cursor.execute("INSERT INTO notes (user, note)
VALUES (?, ?)", ("Alice", "Buy groceries"))
conn.commit()

conn.close()
```

Fetching Data from SQLite

```python
python

conn = sqlite3.connect("notes.db")
cursor = conn.cursor()

cursor.execute("SELECT * FROM notes")
for row in cursor.fetchall():
    print(row)

conn.close()
```

Using SQLAlchemy (More Advanced, Object-Relational Mapping – ORM)

SQLAlchemy allows using **Python classes** to manage databases.

Installing SQLAlchemy:

93

```sh
sh
```

```sh
pip install sqlalchemy
```

Python: Defining a Model with SQLAlchemy

```python
python
```

```python
from sqlalchemy import create_engine, Column, Integer, String
from sqlalchemy.ext.declarative import declarative_base
from sqlalchemy.orm import sessionmaker

Base = declarative_base()

class Note(Base):
    __tablename__ = "notes"
    id = Column(Integer, primary_key=True)
    user = Column(String, nullable=False)
    note = Column(String, nullable=False)

engine = create_engine("sqlite:///notes.db")
Base.metadata.create_all(engine)

Session = sessionmaker(bind=engine)
session = Session()

new_note = Note(user="Alice", note="Call mom")
session.add(new_note)
```

```
session.commit()
```

Querying Data with SQLAlchemy

```
python
```

```python
notes = session.query(Note).all()
for note in notes:
    print(note.user, "-", note.note)
```

Using PostgreSQL (For Large-Scale SQL Databases)

PostgreSQL is used for **enterprise-level applications**.

Installing PostgreSQL Adapter (psycopg2)

```
sh
```

```sh
pip install psycopg2
```

Connecting to PostgreSQL in Python

```
python
```

```python
import psycopg2

conn = psycopg2.connect(
```

95

```
        dbname="mydb",
        user="myuser",
        password="mypassword",
        host="localhost",
        port="5432"
)
cursor = conn.cursor()

cursor.execute("SELECT * FROM users")
print(cursor.fetchall())

conn.close()
```

Using MongoDB (NoSQL Database)

MongoDB stores **JSON-like documents**.

Installing MongoDB Driver (pymongo)

```sh
sh
```

```sh
pip install pymongo
```

Connecting to MongoDB and Inserting a Document

```python
python
```

```python
from pymongo import MongoClient
```

96

```
client                                        =
MongoClient("mongodb://localhost:27017/")
db = client["mydatabase"]
collection = db["notes"]

collection.insert_one({"user": "Alice", "note":
"Read a book"})

for doc in collection.find():
    print(doc)
```

---

3. Connecting to Databases Using C# (Entity Framework Core)

Entity Framework Core (EF Core) simplifies database operations in C#.

Installing EF Core for SQLite:

```sh
dotnet                 add                package
Microsoft.EntityFrameworkCore.Sqlite
```

C#: Defining a Database Model (SQLite Example)

```csharp
```

97

```
using Microsoft.EntityFrameworkCore;
using System;
using System.Linq;

public class Note {
    public int Id { get; set; }
    public string User { get; set; }
    public string Content { get; set; }
}

public class NotesDbContext : DbContext {
    public DbSet<Note> Notes { get; set; }

    protected              override              void
OnConfiguring(DbContextOptionsBuilder options)
        =>                options.UseSqlite("Data
Source=notes.db");
}
```

C#: Inserting Data into SQLite with EF Core

```
csharp

class Program {
    static void Main() {
        using var db = new NotesDbContext();

        db.Database.EnsureCreated();
```

```
        db.Notes.Add(new Note { User = "Alice",
Content = "Buy groceries" });
        db.SaveChanges();
    }
}
```

C#: Fetching Data from SQLite with EF Core

```
csharp
```

```
var notes = db.Notes.ToList();
foreach (var note in notes) {
    Console.WriteLine($"{note.User}:
{note.Content}");
}
```

4. Real-World Example: Multi-User Notes Application

We'll build a **simple note-taking app** that allows users to **add, list, and delete notes**.

Python Version (Using SQLite & SQLAlchemy)

```
python
```

```
from sqlalchemy import create_engine, Column,
Integer, String
```

99

```
from      sqlalchemy.ext.declarative      import
declarative_base
from sqlalchemy.orm import sessionmaker

Base = declarative_base()

class Note(Base):
    __tablename__ = "notes"
    id = Column(Integer, primary_key=True)
    user = Column(String, nullable=False)
    note = Column(String, nullable=False)

engine = create_engine("sqlite:///notes.db")
Base.metadata.create_all(engine)

Session = sessionmaker(bind=engine)
session = Session()

while True:
    command      =      input("Enter      command
(add/list/delete/exit): ").strip().lower()
    if command == "add":
        user = input("Enter your name: ")
        note = input("Enter note: ")
        session.add(Note(user=user, note=note))
        session.commit()
    elif command == "list":
        for note in session.query(Note).all():
```

100

```python
            print(f"{note.id}.        {note.user}:
{note.note}")
    elif command == "delete":
        note_id = int(input("Enter note ID to
delete: "))
        session.query(Note).filter(Note.id    ==
note_id).delete()
        session.commit()
    elif command == "exit":
        break
```

C# Version (Using Entity Framework Core & SQLite)

csharp

```csharp
using System;
using System.Linq;

class Program {
    static void Main() {
        using var db = new NotesDbContext();

        while (true) {
            Console.Write("Enter         command
(add/list/delete/exit): ");
            string          command           =
Console.ReadLine().ToLower();
```

101

```
         if (command == "add") {
             Console.Write("Enter user: ");
             string           user           =
Console.ReadLine();
             Console.Write("Enter note: ");
             string           content         =
Console.ReadLine();

             db.Notes.Add(new Note { User =
user, Content = content });
             db.SaveChanges();
         } else if (command == "list") {
             foreach (var note in db.Notes) {

Console.WriteLine($"{note.Id}.        {note.User}:
{note.Content}");
             }
         } else if (command == "delete") {
             Console.Write("Enter   note   ID:
");
             int            id            =
int.Parse(Console.ReadLine());

             var note = db.Notes.Find(id);
             if      (note      !=      null)
db.Notes.Remove(note);
             db.SaveChanges();
         } else if (command == "exit") {
```

```
        break;
    }
  }
 }
}
```

Conclusion

SQL & NoSQL databases (SQLite, PostgreSQL, MongoDB)

Connecting databases in Python (`sqlite3`, `SQLAlchemy`) and C# (`EF Core`)

Built a multi-user notes app

Next, we'll cover **"Graphical User Interfaces (GUI) Development"** with Python (`Tkinter`) and C# (`WPF`).

CHAPTER 8

GRAPHICAL USER INTERFACES (GUI) DEVELOPMENT

Graphical User Interfaces (GUIs) make applications more user-friendly by allowing interaction through buttons, text fields, and windows instead of command-line input. This chapter covers:

Building desktop apps using Tkinter (Python) and WPF (C#)

Handling user input and events

Deploying GUI apps on Windows, Linux, and macOS

A real-world example: A simple text editor

---

1. Creating Desktop Applications with Tkinter (Python) and WPF (C#)

Tkinter – Python's Built-in GUI Library

Tkinter is a lightweight, cross-platform GUI toolkit that comes with Python.

Installing Tkinter (if not pre-installed)

```sh
sh
```

```sh
pip install tk
```

Creating a Simple Tkinter Window

```python
python

import tkinter as tk

root = tk.Tk()
root.title("My First GUI")
root.geometry("300x200")

label = tk.Label(root, text="Hello, Tkinter!",
font=("Arial", 14))
label.pack(pady=20)

root.mainloop()
```

Output: A small window with "Hello, Tkinter!"

WPF – C#'s GUI Framework for Windows Apps

Windows Presentation Foundation (WPF) is a powerful GUI framework for C#.

Create a New WPF Project:

```sh
sh
```

```
dotnet new wpf -n MyWPFApp
cd MyWPFApp
dotnet run
```

Modify `MainWindow.xaml` to Create a Simple Window

```xml
xml
```

```xml
<Window x:Class="MyWPFApp.MainWindow"

xmlns="http://schemas.microsoft.com/winfx/2006/xaml/presentation"
        Title="My First WPF App" Height="200" Width="300">
    <Grid>
        <TextBlock Text="Hello, WPF!" FontSize="16" HorizontalAlignment="Center" VerticalAlignment="Center"/>
    </Grid>
</Window>
```

Output: A WPF window displaying "Hello, WPF!"

Key Differences:

- **Tkinter (Python)** is simpler but has limited styling.
- **WPF (C#)** allows complex UI designs but is Windows-specific.

---

2. Handling User Input and Events

Handling Button Clicks in Tkinter (Python)

```python
import tkinter as tk

def on_button_click():
    label.config(text="Button Clicked!")

root = tk.Tk()
root.title("Event Handling")

label = tk.Label(root, text="Click the button",
font=("Arial", 14))
label.pack(pady=10)

button = tk.Button(root, text="Click Me",
command=on_button_click)
button.pack()
```

```
root.mainloop()
```

How it works:

- Clicking the button updates the label text using `label.config()`.

Handling Button Clicks in WPF (C#)

Modify `MainWindow.xaml`:

xml

```xml
<Button Content="Click Me" Click="OnButtonClick"
HorizontalAlignment="Center"
VerticalAlignment="Center"/>
```

Modify `MainWindow.xaml.cs`:

csharp

```csharp
using System.Windows;

namespace MyWPFApp {
    public partial class MainWindow : Window {
        public MainWindow() {
            InitializeComponent();
```

```
        }

        private    void     OnButtonClick(object
sender, RoutedEventArgs e) {
            MessageBox.Show("Button Clicked!");
        }
    }
}
```

How it works:

- Clicking the button triggers the `OnButtonClick` method, showing a message box.

---

3. Deploying GUI Apps Across Windows, Linux, and macOS

Packaging a Tkinter App for Distribution

 Convert a Tkinter app into an executable (Windows/macOS/Linux):

sh

```
pip install pyinstaller
pyinstaller --onefile --windowed myapp.py
```

This generates a standalone .exe (Windows) or .app (macOS).

Packaging a WPF App for Windows

Publish as a Standalone Windows App:

```sh
sh
```

```sh
dotnet publish -c Release -r win-x64 --self-contained true
```

This creates a standalone .exe file for distribution.

4. Real-World Example: A Simple Text Editor

Python: Building a Tkinter Text Editor

```python
python
```

```python
import tkinter as tk
from tkinter import filedialog

def open_file():
    file_path = filedialog.askopenfilename()
```

```
    if file_path:
        with open(file_path, "r") as file:
            text_area.delete(1.0, tk.END)
            text_area.insert(tk.END,
file.read())

def save_file():
    file_path                            =
filedialog.asksaveasfilename(defaultextension="
.txt",

filetypes=[("Text    files",    "*.txt"),    ("All
files", "*.*")])
    if file_path:
        with open(file_path, "w") as file:
            file.write(text_area.get(1.0,
tk.END))

root = tk.Tk()
root.title("Simple Text Editor")

text_area = tk.Text(root, wrap="word")
text_area.pack(expand=1, fill="both")

menu = tk.Menu(root)
root.config(menu=menu)

file_menu = tk.Menu(menu, tearoff=0)
menu.add_cascade(label="File", menu=file_menu)
```

111

```
file_menu.add_command(label="Open",
command=open_file)
file_menu.add_command(label="Save",
command=save_file)
file_menu.add_command(label="Exit",
command=root.quit)


root.mainloop()
```

Features: Open, edit, and save text files.

C#: Building a WPF Text Editor

Modify `MainWindow.xaml`:

xml

```
<Grid>
    <DockPancl>
        <Menu DockPanel.Dock="Top">
            <MenuItem Header="File">
                <MenuItem          Header="Open"
Click="OpenFile"/>
                <MenuItem          Header="Save"
Click="SaveFile"/>
                <MenuItem          Header="Exit"
Click="ExitApp"/>
```

```
        </MenuItem>
      </Menu>
      <TextBox                    Name="TextArea"
AcceptsReturn="True"
VerticalScrollBarVisibility="Auto"/>
    </DockPanel>
</Grid>
```

Modify `MainWindow.xaml.cs`:

csharp

```csharp
using System;
using System.IO;
using System.Windows;
using Microsoft.Win32;

namespace TextEditorApp {
    public partial class MainWindow : Window {
        public MainWindow() {
            InitializeComponent();
        }


        private void OpenFile(object sender,
RoutedEventArgs e) {
            OpenFileDialog openFileDialog = new
OpenFileDialog();
            if (openFileDialog.ShowDialog() ==
true) {
```

```
                TextArea.Text                =
File.ReadAllText(openFileDialog.FileName);
            }
        }


        private void SaveFile(object sender,
RoutedEventArgs e) {
            SaveFileDialog saveFileDialog = new
SaveFileDialog();
            if (saveFileDialog.ShowDialog() ==
true) {

File.WriteAllText(saveFileDialog.FileName,
TextArea.Text);
            }
        }


        private void ExitApp(object sender,
RoutedEventArgs e) {
            Application.Current.Shutdown();
        }
    }
}
```

Features: Open, edit, and save text files in a WPF interface.

Conclusion

In this chapter, we learned:

How to create GUI applications using Tkinter (Python) and WPF (C#)

How to handle user input and events

How to package GUI apps for Windows, Linux, and macOS

Built a simple text editor

In the next chapter, we will cover **"Developing Web Applications with Python & C#"** using **Flask (Python) and ASP.NET Core (C#)**.

Shall we proceed with **Chapter 9: Building Web Applications**?

PART 3

WEB AND MOBILE

DEVELOPMENT

CHAPTER 9

BUILDING WEB APPLICATIONS WITH PYTHON & C#

Web applications allow users to interact with **server-side** logic via browsers. In this chapter, we'll explore:
 Introduction to Flask (Python) and ASP.NET MVC (C#)
 Server-side programming: Handling requests and responses
 Real-world example: A personal finance tracker web app

---

1. Introduction to Flask (Python) and ASP.NET MVC (C#)

Flask – Lightweight Web Framework for Python

Flask is a **micro-framework** that allows quick web application development.

Installing Flask:

```sh
sh
```

```
pip install flask
```

Creating a Simple Flask App (app.py)

```
python
```

```
from flask import Flask

app = Flask(__name__)

@app.route("/")
def home():
    return "Hello, Flask!"

if __name__ == "__main__":
    app.run(debug=True)
```

Run the server:

```
sh
```

```
python app.py
```

Visit in a browser:

```
cpp
```

```
http://127.0.0.1:5000/
```

ASP.NET MVC – Robust Web Framework for C#

ASP.NET Core MVC is a **modern web framework** that enables scalable applications.

Create a new ASP.NET MVC project:

```sh

dotnet new mvc -n MyWebApp
cd MyWebApp
dotnet run
```

Modify `Controllers/HomeController.cs` to Add a Route:

```csharp

using Microsoft.AspNetCore.Mvc;

namespace MyWebApp.Controllers {
    public class HomeController : Controller {
        public IActionResult Index() {
            return    Content("Hello,    ASP.NET
MVC!");
        }
    }
}
```

119

Run the server:

```sh
dotnet run
```

Visit in a browser:

```
arduino

http://localhost:5000/
```

Key Differences:

- **Flask (Python)** is simple and great for small projects.
- **ASP.NET MVC (C#)** is structured and better for large applications.

---

2. Server-Side Programming: Handling Requests and Responses

Handling GET and POST Requests in Flask

```python
from flask import Flask, request, jsonify
```

```
app = Flask(__name__)

@app.route("/api/data", methods=["GET", "POST"])
def data():
    if request.method == "POST":
        user_data = request.json
        return    jsonify({"message":    "Data
received", "data": user_data})
    return  jsonify({"message":  "Send  a  POST
request with JSON data"})

if __name__ == "__main__":
    app.run(debug=True)
```

Test with `curl` (POST Request):

sh

```
curl -X POST http://127.0.0.1:5000/api/data -H
"Content-Type:      application/json"      -d
'{"name":"Alice"}'
```

Response:

json

```
{"message":  "Data  received",  "data":  {"name":
"Alice"}}
```

Handling GET and POST Requests in ASP.NET MVC

Modify `Controllers/ApiController.cs`:

csharp

```csharp
using Microsoft.AspNetCore.Mvc;

namespace MyWebApp.Controllers {
    [Route("api")]
    [ApiController]
    public class ApiController : ControllerBase
{
        [HttpGet("data")]
        public IActionResult GetData() {
            return Ok(new { message = "Send a
POST request with JSON data" });
        }

        [HttpPost("data")]
        public IActionResult PostData([FromBody]
dynamic data) {
            return Ok(new { message = "Data
received", data });
        }
    }
}
```

Test with `curl` (POST Request):

```sh
```

```
curl -X POST http://localhost:5000/api/data -H
"Content-Type:        application/json"        -d
'{"name":"Alice"}'
```

Response:

```json
```

```
{"message": "Data received", "data": {"name":
"Alice"}}
```

Key Differences:

- **Flask** uses `request.json` to handle JSON data.
- **ASP.NET MVC** uses `[FromBody]` to deserialize JSON automatically.

3. Real-World Example: Personal Finance Tracker Web App

Features:

User   can   add   income   and   expenses
Database   stores   transactions
Frontend displays current balance

Flask: Personal Finance Tracker

Install dependencies:

sh

```
pip install flask flask-sqlalchemy
```

app.py (Backend API & Database Setup)

python

```
from flask import Flask, request, jsonify
from flask_sqlalchemy import SQLAlchemy

app = Flask(__name__)
app.config["SQLALCHEMY_DATABASE_URI"]          =
"sqlite:///finance.db"
db = SQLAlchemy(app)

class Transaction(db.Model):
    id = db.Column(db.Integer, primary_key=True)
```

```
    type          =          db.Column(db.String(10),
nullable=False)
    amount = db.Column(db.Float, nullable=False)

db.create_all()

@app.route("/transactions",        methods=["GET",
"POST"])
def transactions():
    if request.method == "POST":
        data = request.json
        new_transaction                        =
Transaction(type=data["type"],
amount=data["amount"])
        db.session.add(new_transaction)
        db.session.commit()
        return jsonify({"message": "Transaction
added!"})

    transactions = Transaction.query.all()
    return jsonify([{"type": t.type, "amount":
t.amount} for t in transactions])

if __name__ == "__main__":
    app.run(debug=True)
```

Test API with `curl`:

```sh
sh
```

125

```sh
curl -X POST http://127.0.0.1:5000/transactions
-H "Content-Type: application/json" -d
'{"type":"income","amount":1000}'
```

Fetching Transactions:

```sh
sh
```

```sh
curl -X GET http://127.0.0.1:5000/transactions
```

ASP.NET MVC: Personal Finance Tracker

Install dependencies:

```sh
sh
```

```sh
dotnet add package
Microsoft.EntityFrameworkCore.Sqlite
```

Models/Transaction.cs (Database Model)

```csharp
csharp

using System.ComponentModel.DataAnnotations;

public class Transaction {
    [Key]
    public int Id { get; set; }
    public string Type { get; set; }
```

126

```csharp
    public double Amount { get; set; }
}
```

Controllers/FinanceController.cs (API Endpoints)

csharp

```csharp
using Microsoft.AspNetCore.Mvc;
using System.Collections.Generic;
using System.Linq;

namespace MyWebApp.Controllers {
    [Route("api")]
    [ApiController]
    public class FinanceController :
ControllerBase {
        private static List<Transaction>
transactions = new List<Transaction>();

        [HttpGet("transactions")]
        public IActionResult GetTransactions() {
            return Ok(transactions);
        }

        [HttpPost("transactions")]
        public                        IActionResult
AddTransaction([FromBody]          Transaction
transaction) {
            transactions.Add(transaction);
```

```
        return    Ok(new    {    message    =
"Transaction added!" });
        }
    }
}
```

Test API with `curl`:

sh

```
curl                    -X                    POST
http://localhost:5000/api/transactions      -H
"Content-Type:        application/json"      -d
'{"type":"income","amount":1000}'
```

Fetching Transactions:

sh

```
curl                    -X                    GET
http://localhost:5000/api/transactions
```

Conclusion

In this chapter, we built web applications with: **Flask (Python) and ASP.NET MVC (C#) Handled GET and POST requests Developed a Personal Finance Tracker API**

128

In the next chapter, we will explore **"Developing Mobile Apps Using Python & C#"** using **Kivy (Python) and Xamarin (C#)**.

Shall we proceed with **Chapter 10: Developing Mobile Apps**?

CHAPTER 10

DEVELOPING MOBILE APPS
USING PYTHON & C#

Building mobile applications for **iOS** and **Android** requires cross-platform frameworks that enable developers to write code once and deploy it everywhere. This chapter covers:

Cross-platform mobile frameworks: Kivy (Python) and Xamarin   (C#)

Creating   simple   mobile   UI   elements

Handling device-specific features (camera, location, storage)

A real-world example: A to-do list mobile app

---

1. Cross-Platform Mobile Frameworks: Kivy (Python) and Xamarin (C#)

Kivy – Python's Cross-Platform Mobile Framework

Kivy is an open-source framework that allows building mobile applications with **Python**. It supports **iOS, Android, Windows, Linux, and macOS**.

Installing Kivy:

```sh
pip install kivy
```

Create a basic Kivy app (`main.py`):

```python
from kivy.app import App
from kivy.uix.label import Label

class MyApp(App):
    def build(self):
        return Label(text="Hello, Kivy!")

if __name__ == "__main__":
    MyApp().run()
```

Run the app:

```sh
python main.py
```

Advantages of Kivy:

- **Python-based:** Leverages Python's simplicity.
- **Multi-touch support:** Works well for touchscreens.
- **Cross-platform:** Runs on **Android, iOS, Windows, macOS, and Linux**.

Xamarin – C#'s Cross-Platform Mobile Framework

Xamarin (powered by .NET MAUI) is **Microsoft's** cross-platform framework for **Android and iOS** development.

Create a Xamarin Project:

```sh
```

```sh
dotnet new maui -n MyXamarinApp
cd MyXamarinApp
dotnet build
dotnet run
```

Modify `MainPage.xaml` (UI Layout):

```xml
```

```
<ContentPage
xmlns="http://schemas.microsoft.com/dotnet/2021
/maui"
            x:Class="MyXamarinApp.MainPage">
    <VerticalStackLayout>
        <Label        Text="Hello,        Xamarin!"
FontSize="24" HorizontalOptions="Center"/>
    </VerticalStackLayout>
</ContentPage>
```

Advantages of Xamarin:

- **Native Performance:** Apps run as native Android/iOS apps.
- **C# Codebase:** Uses C#, making it ideal for .NET developers.
- **Access to Native APIs:** Easily interact with **camera, GPS, and sensors**.

2. Creating Simple Mobile UI Elements

Kivy: Buttons and Text Input Example

```python

from kivy.app import App
from kivy.uix.boxlayout import BoxLayout
```

```
from kivy.uix.button import Button
from kivy.uix.textinput import TextInput

class MyApp(App):
    def build(self):
        layout                            =
BoxLayout(orientation="vertical")

        self.text_input                   =
TextInput(hint_text="Enter text")
        layout.add_widget(self.text_input)

        button = Button(text="Click Me")

button.bind(on_press=self.on_button_click)
        layout.add_widget(button)

        return layout

    def on_button_click(self, instance):
        print(f"Button      Clicked!      Input:
{self.text_input.text}")

if __name__ == "__main__":
    MyApp().run()
```

Features:

A   text   input   field
A button that prints input on click

134

Xamarin: Buttons and Text Input Example (`MainPage.xaml`)

xml

```
<ContentPage
xmlns="http://schemas.microsoft.com/dotnet/2021
/maui"
            x:Class="MyXamarinApp.MainPage">
    <VerticalStackLayout>
        <Entry              x:Name="textInput"
Placeholder="Enter text"/>
        <Button         Text="Click         Me"
Clicked="OnButtonClick"/>
        <Label x:Name="outputLabel"/>
    </VerticalStackLayout>
</ContentPage>
```

Modify `MainPage.xaml.cs`:

csharp

```
using Microsoft.Maui.Controls;

namespace MyXamarinApp {
    public partial class MainPage : ContentPage
{
```

```
public MainPage() {
    InitializeComponent();
}


private    void    OnButtonClick(object
sender, EventArgs e) {
    outputLabel.Text = "Button Clicked!
Input: " + textInput.Text;
    }
  }
}
```

Features:

A   text   field   for   user   input

A button that updates the label on click

---

3. Handling Device-Specific Features (Camera, Location, Storage)

Accessing the Camera in Kivy

Install pyjnius for Android camera access:

```sh
sh

pip install pyjnius
```

Capture an Image (Android only):

python

```
from jnius import autoclass

Camera = autoclass("android.hardware.Camera")
camera = Camera.open()
camera.startPreview()
```

For iOS, use Kivy-iOS with `plyer` for camera access.

Accessing the Camera in Xamarin (C#)

Install Xamarin.Essentials:

sh

```
dotnet add package Xamarin.Essentials
```

Take a Picture in Xamarin (`MainPage.xaml.cs`):

csharp

```csharp
using Xamarin.Essentials;
using System;
using Microsoft.Maui.Controls;
```

137

```
public   async   void   TakePhoto(object   sender,
EventArgs e) {
    var            photo          =          await
MediaPicker.CapturePhotoAsync();
    if (photo != null) {
        var         stream        =          await
photo.OpenReadAsync();
        imageView.Source                        =
ImageSource.FromStream(() => stream);
    }
}
```

Xamarin provides built-in support for accessing the camera.

Getting GPS Location in Kivy

```
python

from plyer import gps

def get_location():
    gps.configure(on_location=lambda   **kwargs:
print(kwargs))
    gps.start()
```

Plyer provides access to mobile features like GPS and notifications.

Getting GPS Location in Xamarin (C#)

```csharp
using Xamarin.Essentials;

var location = await Geolocation.GetLastKnownLocationAsync();
Console.WriteLine($"Latitude: {location.Latitude}, Longitude: {location.Longitude}");
```

Xamarin.Essentials provides cross-platform access to sensors.

---

4. Real-World Example: A To-Do List Mobile App

Kivy: To-Do List App

```python
from kivy.app import App
```

```python
from kivy.uix.boxlayout import BoxLayout
from kivy.uix.textinput import TextInput
from kivy.uix.button import Button
from kivy.uix.label import Label

class ToDoApp(App):
    def build(self):
        self.layout                          =
BoxLayout(orientation="vertical")
        self.task_input                      =
TextInput(hint_text="Enter task")
        self.layout.add_widget(self.task_input)

        self.task_list                       =
BoxLayout(orientation="vertical")
        self.layout.add_widget(self.task_list)

        add_button = Button(text="Add Task")
        add_button.bind(on_press=self.add_task)
        self.layout.add_widget(add_button)

        return self.layout

    def add_task(self, instance):
        task_text = self.task_input.text
        task_label = Label(text=task_text)
        self.task_list.add_widget(task_label)
        self.task_input.text = ""
```

```
if __name__ == "__main__":
    ToDoApp().run()
```

Xamarin: To-Do List App (`MainPage.xaml`)

xml

```xml
<StackLayout>
    <Entry x:Name="taskInput" Placeholder="Enter task"/>
    <Button Text="Add Task" Clicked="AddTask"/>
    <ListView x:Name="taskList"/>
</StackLayout>
```

Modify `MainPage.xaml.cs`:

csharp

```csharp
using System;
using System.Collections.ObjectModel;
using Microsoft.Maui.Controls;

public partial class MainPage : ContentPage {
    ObservableCollection<string> tasks = new ObservableCollection<string>();

    public MainPage() {
        InitializeComponent();
```

```
        taskList.ItemsSource = tasks;
    }


    private    void    AddTask(object    sender,
EventArgs e) {
        if
(!string.IsNullOrWhiteSpace(taskInput.Text)) {
            tasks.Add(taskInput.Text);
            taskInput.Text = "";
        }
    }
}
```

Conclusion

In   this   chapter,   we:

Explored Kivy (Python) and Xamarin (C#) for mobile development

Built   UI   elements   for   user   interaction

Accessed   device-specific   features   (camera,   GPS, storage)

Built a To-Do List mobile app

Next, we will cover **"Using Blazor and WebAssembly for Cross-Platform Apps"**.

Shall we proceed with **Chapter 11: Blazor and WebAssembly**?

CHAPTER 11

USING BLAZOR AND WEBASSEMBLY FOR CROSS-PLATFORM APPS

Blazor and WebAssembly bring the power of **C# to the browser**, enabling developers to build **modern, high-performance web applications** without relying on JavaScript. In this chapter, we'll cover: **Introduction to Blazor (C#) and WebAssembly Running C# in the browser Connecting Blazor with Python backend services A real-world example: A stock price tracking dashboard**

---

1. Introduction to Blazor (C#) and WebAssembly

What is Blazor?

Blazor is a web framework that allows **C# developers to build interactive web applications** using Razor components. It provides two hosting models:

Hosting Model	Description
Blazor WebAssembly (WASM)	Runs C# code **directly in the browser** via WebAssembly.
Blazor Server	Runs on the server and updates UI via **SignalR** (faster initial load).

We will focus on Blazor WebAssembly since it enables full **cross-platform** capabilities.

What is WebAssembly?

WebAssembly (**WASM**) is a binary instruction format that allows running **compiled code (C, C++, Rust, C#) inside the** **browser**.
Faster **than** **JavaScript**
Runs **natively** **in** **the** **browser**
Cross-platform (Windows, macOS, Linux, Mobile)

Blazor WebAssembly **compiles C# into WebAssembly**, allowing it to run **directly in the browser** without a backend server.

---

2. Running C# in the Browser with Blazor WebAssembly

Setting Up a Blazor WebAssembly Project

Install .NET SDK (if not installed):

sh

```
dotnet --version   # Check .NET SDK version
```

Create a Blazor WebAssembly project:

sh

```
dotnet new blazorwasm -n MyBlazorApp
cd MyBlazorApp
dotnet run
```

Visit in a browser:

arduino

```
http://localhost:5000/
```

Understanding Blazor Components

Blazor apps are built with **Razor Components** (.razor files).

146

Modify `Pages/Index.razor` to Display a Counter:

razor

```
@page "/"
<h3>Welcome to Blazor WebAssembly</h3>
<p>Counter: @count</p>
<button @onclick="Increment">Click Me</button>

@code {
    private int count = 0;
    private void Increment() {
        count++;
    }
}
```

Key   Features:

Uses **C# for event handling** (`@onclick="Increment"`)

No   need   for   JavaScript

Runs entirely in the browser

---

3. Connecting Blazor with Python Backend Services

While **Blazor WebAssembly runs in the browser**, it often needs to interact with a **backend API**. Here, we'll connect **Blazor (C# frontend)** with a **Flask (Python backend)**.

147

Step 1: Set Up a Flask API (Python Backend)

Install Flask & Flask-CORS (for cross-origin requests):

```sh
pip install flask flask-cors
```

Create a Simple Flask API (`app.py`):

```python
from flask import Flask, jsonify
from flask_cors import CORS

app = Flask(__name__)
CORS(app)  # Allow Blazor to access the API

@app.route("/api/stock", methods=["GET"])
def get_stock():
    return jsonify({"symbol": "AAPL", "price": 145.32})

if __name__ == "__main__":
    app.run(debug=True)
```

Run the Flask API:

```sh
sh
```

```
python app.py
```

This API provides real-time stock price data for Blazor.

Step 2: Fetch API Data in Blazor

Modify `Pages/Stock.razor` to fetch stock prices from Flask.

```razor
razor
```

```razor
@page "/stock"
<h3>Stock Price Tracker</h3>
<p>Stock Symbol: @symbol</p>
<p>Current Price: @price USD</p>
<button
@onclick="FetchStockData">Refresh</button>

@code {
    private string symbol = "";
    private decimal price = 0;

    private async Task FetchStockData() {
        var http = new HttpClient();
```

```
        var      response      =      await
http.GetFromJsonAsync<StockData>("http://127.0.
0.1:5000/api/stock");
        if (response != null) {
            symbol = response.Symbol;
            price = response.Price;
        }
    }


    public class StockData {
        public string Symbol { get; set; }
        public decimal Price { get; set; }
    }
}
```

How   it   works:
Fetches stock prices from the **Flask API** using `HttpClient`
Updates the UI dynamically **without reloading the page**

---

4. Real-World Example: A Stock Price Tracking
Dashboard

We will enhance the **Stock Price Tracker** with:
Live   price   updates every   5   seconds
Data visualization with a chart

150

Modify `Pages/StockDashboard.razor`

razor

```razor
@page "/stock-dashboard"
@inject HttpClient Http

<h3>Live Stock Price Tracker</h3>
<p>Stock Symbol: @symbol</p>
<p>Current Price: @price USD</p>
<button
@onclick="FetchStockData">Refresh</button>

<canvas id="stockChart"></canvas>

@code {
    private string symbol = "AAPL";
    private decimal price = 0;
    private Timer _timer;

    protected     override     async     Task
OnInitializedAsync() {
        await FetchStockData();
        _timer = new Timer(async _ => await
FetchStockData(), null, 0, 5000);
    }
```

```
private async Task FetchStockData() {
    var        response      =        await
Http.GetFromJsonAsync<StockData>("http://127.0.
0.1:5000/api/stock");
        if (response != null) {
            symbol = response.Symbol;
            price = response.Price;
            await UpdateChart();
        }
    }


    private async Task UpdateChart() {
        await
JS.InvokeVoidAsync("updateStockChart", price);
    }


    public class StockData {
        public string Symbol { get; set; }
        public decimal Price { get; set; }
    }
}
```

Modify wwwroot/index.html to Include a JavaScript Chart

```
html
```

```
<script
src="https://cdn.jsdelivr.net/npm/chart.js"></s
cript>
<script>
    var stockChart;
    function updateStockChart(price) {
        if (!stockChart) {
            var              ctx              =
document.getElementById('stockChart').getContex
t('2d');
            stockChart = new Chart(ctx, {
                type: 'line',
                data: {
                    labels: [],
                    datasets: [{
                        label: 'Stock Price',
                        data: [],
                        borderColor: 'blue',
                        borderWidth: 2
                    }]
                }
            });
        }
        stockChart.data.labels.push(new
Date().toLocaleTimeString());

stockChart.data.datasets[0].data.push(price);
        stockChart.update();
    }
```

```
</script>
```

Key **Features:**

Fetches **live** **stock** **prices** every 5 seconds

Updates **UI** **dynamically**

Uses **Chart.js for visualization**

Conclusion

In this chapter, we:

Explored Blazor WebAssembly for cross-platform C# apps

Ran C# code in the browser

Connected Blazor with a Flask (Python) backend

Built a real-world stock price tracking dashboard

In the next chapter, we will explore **Asynchronous Programming and Multithreading** to improve app performance.

Shall we proceed with **Chapter 12: Asynchronous Programming and Multithreading**?

CHAPTER 12

ASYNCHRONOUS PROGRAMMING AND MULTITHREADING

Modern applications often need to perform multiple tasks simultaneously, such as **downloading files, fetching API data, or running background computations**. In this chapter, we'll explore:

Async and Await in C#

Multithreading in Python with `asyncio`

When to use multithreading vs multiprocessing

A real-world example: A concurrent file downloader

---

1. Async and Await in C#

C# provides built-in support for **asynchronous programming** using `async` and `await`.

Why Use Async?

- **Prevents blocking the main thread** (better performance).
- **Ideal for I/O operations** like API calls, file reading, and database queries.
- **Improves UI responsiveness** in desktop and mobile apps.

Basic Example of Async and Await in C#

```csharp
using System;
using System.Net.Http;
using System.Threading.Tasks;

class Program {
    static async Task Main() {
        Console.WriteLine("Fetching data...");
        string data = await FetchData();
        Console.WriteLine($"Received: {data}");
    }

    static async Task<string> FetchData() {
        using HttpClient client = new HttpClient();
```

```
        return                              await
client.GetStringAsync("https://jsonplaceholder.
typicode.com/todos/1");
    }
}
```

How **it** **works:**

`async` tells the compiler that the method will run asynchronously.

`await` waits for the HTTP request **without blocking the main thread**.

Running Multiple Async Tasks in Parallel

csharp

```
using System;
using System.Net.Http;
using System.Threading.Tasks;

class Program {
    static async Task Main() {
        Console.WriteLine("Fetching      multiple
tasks...");
```

```
        Task<string>          task1          =
FetchData("https://jsonplaceholder.typicode.com
/todos/1");
        Task<string>          task2          =
FetchData("https://jsonplaceholder.typicode.com
/todos/2");

        string[]      results      =      await
Task.WhenAll(task1, task2);

        Console.WriteLine("Task  1  Result:  "  +
results[0]);
        Console.WriteLine("Task  2  Result:  "  +
results[1]);
    }

    static  async  Task<string>  FetchData(string
url) {
        using     HttpClient     client     =     new
HttpClient();
        return await client.GetStringAsync(url);
    }
}
```

How   it   works:

`Task.WhenAll(task1,  task2)` executes both tasks in parallel.

Reduces execution time significantly compared to running tasks sequentially.

158

2. Multithreading in Python with `asyncio`

Python provides `asyncio` for **asynchronous programming** and `threading` for **multithreading**.

Basic Async/Await Example in Python (`asyncio`)

python

```python
import asyncio

async def fetch_data():
    print("Fetching data...")
    await asyncio.sleep(2)   # Simulate network delay
    return "Data received!"

async def main():
    data = await fetch_data()
    print(data)

asyncio.run(main())
```

How it works:
`await asyncio.sleep(2)` simulates an **asynchronous**

159

delay.

Does not block other tasks while waiting.

Running Multiple Async Tasks in Parallel

python

```python
import asyncio

async def fetch_data(id):
    print(f"Fetching data {id}...")
    await asyncio.sleep(2)
    return f"Data {id} received!"

async def main():
    tasks = [fetch_data(1), fetch_data(2)]
    results = await asyncio.gather(*tasks)

    for result in results:
        print(result)

asyncio.run(main())
```

How **it** **works:**

`asyncio.gather(*tasks)` runs both tasks **concurrently**.

Executes faster than running them sequentially.

3. When to Use Multithreading vs Multiprocessing

Feature	Multithreading	Multiprocessing
Best for	I/O-bound tasks (network, file I/O)	CPU-bound tasks (image processing, computations)
Uses	Threads (shared memory)	Separate processes (independent memory)
Example	Downloading multiple files	Performing machine learning training

Python: Multithreading Example (I/O Bound)

```python
python

import threading
import time

def task(name):
    print(f"Starting {name}")
    time.sleep(2)  # Simulate I/O delay
    print(f"Completed {name}")

thread1    =    threading.Thread(target=task,
args=("Task 1",))
```

161

```
thread2          =          threading.Thread(target=task,
args=("Task 2",))

thread1.start()
thread2.start()

thread1.join()
thread2.join()
```

When to use? When dealing with **file operations, API requests, or database queries**.

Python: Multiprocessing Example (CPU Bound)

```python
import multiprocessing

def compute(n):
    return sum(i * i for i in range(n))

if __name__ == "__main__":
    with multiprocessing.Pool(4) as pool:
        results = pool.map(compute, [10**6,
10**6, 10**6, 10**6])
        print(results)
```

When to use? When dealing with **CPU-intensive tasks** like **image processing, cryptography, or deep learning**.

---

4. Real-World Example: A Concurrent File Downloader

In this example, we will build a **parallel file downloader** using:

`asyncio` in **Python**

`async/await` in C#

Python: Asynchronous File Downloader

```python
python

import asyncio
import aiohttp
import aiofiles

async def download_file(url, filename):
    async with aiohttp.ClientSession() as session:
        async with session.get(url) as response:
            if response.status == 200:
```

```
            async                    with
aiofiles.open(filename, 'wb') as file:
                await        file.write(await
response.read())
            print(f"Downloaded {filename}")

async def main():
    urls = [
        ("https://example.com/file1.txt",
"file1.txt"),
        ("https://example.com/file2.txt",
"file2.txt"),
    ]
    tasks = [download_file(url, filename) for
url, filename in urls]
    await asyncio.gather(*tasks)

asyncio.run(main())
```

How   it   works:
Uses **aiohttp** for **async HTTP requests**.
Downloads multiple files **concurrently**.

C#: Asynchronous File Downloader

```
csharp
```

164

```csharp
using System;
using System.IO;
using System.Net.Http;
using System.Threading.Tasks;

class Program {
    static async Task Main() {
        string[] urls = {
            "https://example.com/file1.txt",
            "https://example.com/file2.txt"
        };

        Task[] tasks = new Task[urls.Length];

        for (int i = 0; i < urls.Length; i++) {
            tasks[i]    =    DownloadFile(urls[i],
$"file{i+1}.txt");
        }

        await Task.WhenAll(tasks);
    }

    static async Task DownloadFile(string url,
string filename) {
        using    HttpClient    client    =    new
HttpClient();
        byte[]        fileData        =        await
client.GetByteArrayAsync(url);
```

```
        await File.WriteAllBytesAsync(filename,
fileData);
        Console.WriteLine($"Downloaded
{filename}");
    }
}
```

How it works:
Uses `HttpClient.GetByteArrayAsync(url)` for **non-blocking downloads**.
Uses `Task.WhenAll(tasks)` to **download multiple files simultaneously**.

Conclusion

In this chapter, we:
Explored **Async/Await in C#** for **non-blocking tasks**
Used **asyncio** in Python for **asynchronous programming**
Compared **multithreading vs multiprocessing**
Built a **concurrent file downloader**

In the next chapter, we'll explore **"Interoperability: Running Python in C# and Vice Versa"**, where we'll combine Python's flexibility with C#'s performance.

Shall we proceed with **Chapter 13: Interoperability – Running Python in C# and Vice Versa**?

CHAPTER 13

INTEROPERABILITY – RUNNING PYTHON IN C# AND VICE VERSA

Modern applications often leverage multiple languages to combine their strengths. Python is **great for AI/ML, data processing, and scripting**, while C# **excels at high-performance applications, GUI development, and enterprise systems**. This chapter explores: **Calling Python scripts from C# using Python.NET Calling C# libraries from Python using** `pycsharp` **A real-world example: Running a machine learning model in Python from a C# desktop app**

---

1. Calling Python Scripts from C# using Python.NET

Python.NET (`pythonnet`) allows **embedding Python inside C# applications** and calling Python functions directly.

Installing Python.NET

First, install **Python.NET** in Python:

```sh
pip install pythonnet
```

Running a Python Script from C#

Let's assume we have a **Python script** (`ml_model.py`) that performs a simple operation.

Create `ml_model.py`

```python
def predict(number):
    return number * 2  # Simulated ML prediction
```

Run `ml_model.py` from C#

```csharp
using System;
using Python.Runtime;  // Import Python.NET

class Program {
    static void Main() {
```

```
        PythonEngine.Initialize();              //
Initialize Python Runtime


        using (Py.GIL()) {   // Acquire Global
Interpreter Lock
            dynamic ml = Py.Import("ml_model");
// Import Python script
            int result = ml.predict(5);  // Call
the Python function
            Console.WriteLine($"ML   Prediction:
{result}");
        }


        PythonEngine.Shutdown();    //  Shutdown
Python Runtime
    }
}
```

Output:

yaml

ML Prediction: 10

Key   Concepts:

`PythonEngine.Initialize()` starts the Python runtime inside C#.

`Py.Import("ml_model")` loads the Python script.

`using (Py.GIL())` ensures **thread safety** when calling

170

Python.

`PythonEngine.Shutdown()` properly releases Python resources.

---

2. Calling C# Libraries from Python Using `pycsharp`

To use C# libraries in Python, we can: **Compile a .NET DLL** and load it in Python. Use `clr` from **Python.NET** for direct calls.

Creating a C# DLL for Python

Step 1: Create a C# Class Library

```sh
```

```sh
dotnet new classlib -n MyCSharpLibrary
cd MyCSharpLibrary
```

Step 2: Modify `Class1.cs` to Define a Function

```csharp
```

```csharp
namespace MyCSharpLibrary {
```

171

```
public class Calculator {
    public int Add(int a, int b) {
        return a + b;
    }
}
}
```

Step 3: Build the C# Library

sh

dotnet build

This creates a `MyCSharpLibrary.dll` file inside the `bin/Debug/netstandard2.0/` folder.

Calling C# from Python Using `clr`

First, install **Python.NET** (if not already installed):

sh

pip install pythonnet

Run C# Code in Python (`call_csharp.py`)

python

```
import clr

# Load the C# DLL
clr.AddReference(r"bin/Debug/netstandard2.0/MyC
SharpLibrary.dll")

# Import the C# namespace
from MyCSharpLibrary import Calculator

# Use the C# function
calc = Calculator()
result = calc.Add(3, 7)
print(f"Result from C#: {result}")
```

Output:

```
csharp

Result from C#: 10
```

Key   **Concepts:**

`clr.AddReference("MyCSharpLibrary.dll")` loads the C#   DLL.

`from MyCSharpLibrary import Calculator` accesses C# classes.

Works with **Windows, macOS, and Linux** if .NET is installed.

173

3. Real-World Example: Running a Machine Learning Model in Python Inside a C# Desktop App

Let's integrate **a Python ML model into a C# WPF desktop app**.

Step 1: Create a Python ML Model (`ml_model.py`)

```python
python

import numpy as np
import joblib

# Train a simple model
X = np.array([1, 2, 3, 4, 5]).reshape(-1, 1)
y = np.array([2, 4, 6, 8, 10])
from         sklearn.linear_model         import
LinearRegression

model = LinearRegression()
model.fit(X, y)
joblib.dump(model, "model.pkl")   # Save model
```

This saves a trained ML model (`model.pkl`).

174

Step 2: Create a Python Script for C# to Call (`ml_predict.py`)

```python
python

import joblib

model = joblib.load("model.pkl")  # Load ML model

def predict(number):
    return float(model.predict([[number]])[0])
```

Step 3: Create a C# WPF Application That Calls Python

Modify `MainWindow.xaml` to add a **button and text box**:

```xml
xml

<Window x:Class="MLApp.MainWindow"

xmlns="http://schemas.microsoft.com/winfx/2006/
xaml/presentation"
        Title="ML    Predictor"    Height="200"
Width="300">
    <Grid>
        <StackPanel>
```

175

```
        <TextBox           x:Name="inputBox"
PlaceholderText="Enter a number"/>
        <Button            Content="Predict"
Click="Predict_Click"/>
        <TextBlock x:Name="outputLabel"/>
      </StackPanel>
   </Grid>
</Window>
```

Modify `MainWindow.xaml.cs` to **call the Python ML model**:

csharp

```
using System;
using System.Diagnostics;
using System.Windows;

namespace MLApp {
    public partial class MainWindow : Window {
        public MainWindow() {
            InitializeComponent();
        }

        private void Predict_Click(object
sender, RoutedEventArgs e) {
            string input = inputBox.Text;
            string         result         =
RunPythonScript(input);
```

```
        outputLabel.Text = "Prediction: " +
result;
    }


    private   string   RunPythonScript(string
input) {
        ProcessStartInfo   psi   =   new
ProcessStartInfo {
            FileName = "python",
            Arguments   =   $"ml_predict.py
{input}",
            RedirectStandardOutput = true,
            UseShellExecute = false,
            CreateNoWindow = true
        };


        Process         process         =
Process.Start(psi);
        process.WaitForExit();
        return
process.StandardOutput.ReadToEnd().Trim();
    }
  }
}
```

Key   Features:
Runs a Python ML model inside a C# WPF application.
Executes Python scripts via `ProcessStartInfo` and
reads output.

Step 4: Run the C# App and Enter a Number

Input: 5

Output: Prediction: 10.0

Conclusion

In   this   chapter,   we:

Called Python scripts from C# using Python.NET

Called C# libraries from Python using `clr`

Built a real-world ML-powered C# WPF application

Next, we'll explore **"Machine Learning and AI Integration"**, where we will **deploy AI models in cross-platform applications**.

Shall we proceed with **Chapter 14: Machine Learning and AI Integration**?

CHAPTER 14

MACHINE LEARNING AND AI INTEGRATION

Artificial Intelligence (AI) and Machine Learning (ML) have transformed how applications work by enabling automation, decision-making, and predictive capabilities. This chapter covers:

Basics of AI and ML in Python (TensorFlow, Scikit-learn)

Using ML models inside C# applications
A real-world example: Image recognition software

---

1. Basics of AI and ML in Python (TensorFlow, Scikit-learn)

Python is the **primary language** for AI and ML due to its vast ecosystem of libraries, such as:

- **TensorFlow & Keras** → Deep learning
- **Scikit-learn** → Traditional ML algorithms
- **OpenCV** → Computer vision

- **Pandas & NumPy** → Data manipulation

Creating a Simple Machine Learning Model (Scikit-learn)

Let's build a **basic linear regression model** that predicts house prices based on area size.

Step 1: Install Dependencies
sh

```
pip install numpy pandas scikit-learn joblib
```

Step 2: Train a Regression Model (train_model.py)
python

```
import numpy as np
import joblib
from       sklearn.linear_model       import
LinearRegression

# Training Data (Area in sq ft -> Price in $1000s)
X   =   np.array([500,   700,   1000,   1200,
1500]).reshape(-1, 1)
y = np.array([150, 200, 250, 280, 320])

# Train model
```

```
model = LinearRegression()
model.fit(X, y)

# Save model
joblib.dump(model, "house_price_model.pkl")
print("Model trained and saved!")
```

What   happens   here?

The model learns a **linear relationship** between house size
and   price.

Saves the trained model as house_price_model.pkl.

Using the Trained Model to Make Predictions

Step 3: Create a Python Script to Use the Model (predict.py)
```
python

import sys
import joblib

# Load trained model
model = joblib.load("house_price_model.pkl")

# Get input from C#
size = float(sys.argv[1])  # Input from command
line
predicted_price = model.predict([[size]])[0]
```

```
# Print result (for C# to read)
print(predicted_price)
```

This **script:**
Loads the trained ML model. Accepts **input from C# via command-line arguments**. Outputs a prediction for **C# to capture**.

---

2. Using ML Models Inside C# Applications

Now, let's call the **Python ML model** inside a C# **desktop** app.

Step 1: Create a C# WPF App and Modify `MainWindow.xaml`

xml

```
<Window x:Class="MLApp.MainWindow"

xmlns="http://schemas.microsoft.com/winfx/2006/
xaml/presentation"
        Title="House       Price        Predictor"
Height="200" Width="300">
    <Grid>
        <StackPanel>
```

```
        <TextBox              x:Name="inputBox"
PlaceholderText="Enter house size (sq ft)"/>
        <Button    Content="Predict    Price"
Click="Predict_Click"/>
        <TextBlock x:Name="outputLabel"/>
    </StackPanel>
  </Grid>
</Window>
```

Step 2: Modify `MainWindow.xaml.cs` to Call the Python ML Model

csharp

```csharp
using System;
using System.Diagnostics;
using System.Windows;

namespace MLApp {
    public partial class MainWindow : Window {
        public MainWindow() {
            InitializeComponent();
        }

        private    void    Predict_Click(object
sender, RoutedEventArgs e) {
            string input = inputBox.Text;
```

```
        string          result          =
RunPythonScript(input);
        outputLabel.Text = "Predicted Price:
$" + result + "K";
    }


    private  string  RunPythonScript(string
input) {
        ProcessStartInfo   psi   =   new
ProcessStartInfo {
            FileName = "python",
            Arguments    =    $"predict.py
{input}",
            RedirectStandardOutput = true,
            UseShellExecute = false,
            CreateNoWindow = true
        };


        Process          process          =
Process.Start(psi);
        process.WaitForExit();
        return
process.StandardOutput.ReadToEnd().Trim();
    }
  }
}
```

How   it   Works:
Calls   the   **Python   ML   model**   from   C#.

Passes the house size **as a command-line argument**.
Reads **the ML model's prediction** and displays it in the UI.

Running the C# Application

Train the model (only once):

```sh
python train_model.py
```

Run the WPF C# App and enter:

```yaml
1200
```

Output:

```nginx
Predicted Price: $280K
```

185

3. Real-World Example: Image Recognition Software

Now, let's integrate **an image recognition model** inside a C# desktop app.

Step 1: Train a Simple Image Classification Model in Python

sh

```
pip install tensorflow keras numpy opencv-python
joblib
python

import tensorflow as tf
from tensorflow import keras
import numpy as np
import cv2
import joblib

# Load pre-trained model (MobileNetV2)
model                                          =
keras.applications.MobileNetV2(weights="imagene
t")

# Function to make a prediction
def predict_image(image_path):
```

```
    image = cv2.imread(image_path)
    image = cv2.resize(image, (224, 224))    #
Resize for model
    image = np.expand_dims(image, axis=0) / 255.0
# Normalize
    preds = model.predict(image)
    decoded_preds                            =
keras.applications.mobilenet_v2.decode_predicti
ons(preds, top=1)[0]
    return  decoded_preds[0][1]       #   Return
predicted class


# Save function for C# to call
joblib.dump(predict_image,
"image_classifier.pkl")
```

This   script:

Uses a pre-trained **MobileNetV2 model** for image recognition.

Saves the prediction function inside **image_classifier.pkl**.

Step 2: Create a Python Script to Run Predictions (`image_predict.py`)

```
python
```

187

```python
import sys
import joblib

predict_fn = joblib.load("image_classifier.pkl")
image_path = sys.argv[1]
result = predict_fn(image_path)

print(result)
```

Step 3: Modify the C# WPF App to Call the Python Model

Modify `MainWindow.xaml` to allow **image selection**:

xml

```xml
<Grid>
    <StackPanel>
        <Button Content="Select Image" Click="SelectImage"/>
        <Image x:Name="displayImage" Height="200"/>
        <Button Content="Predict" Click="Predict_Click"/>
        <TextBlock x:Name="outputLabel"/>
    </StackPanel>
</Grid>
```

188

Modify `MainWindow.xaml.cs` to **call the Python image classifier**:

csharp

```csharp
using System;
using System.Diagnostics;
using System.Windows;
using Microsoft.Win32;

namespace MLApp {
    public partial class MainWindow : Window {
        private string selectedImagePath = "";

        public MainWindow() {
            InitializeComponent();
        }

        private void SelectImage(object sender,
RoutedEventArgs e) {
            OpenFileDialog    dialog    =    new
OpenFileDialog { Filter = "Images|*.jpg;*.png" };
            if (dialog.ShowDialog() == true) {
                selectedImagePath           =
dialog.FileName;
                displayImage.Source    =    new
BitmapImage(new Uri(selectedImagePath));
            }
        }
```

```
        private     void     Predict_Click(object
sender, RoutedEventArgs e) {
            if
(string.IsNullOrEmpty(selectedImagePath)) {
                outputLabel.Text  =  "Select  an
image first!";
                return;
            }

            string            result            =
RunPythonScript(selectedImagePath);
            outputLabel.Text = "Prediction: " +
result;
        }


        private   string   RunPythonScript(string
imagePath) {
            ProcessStartInfo    psi    =    new
ProcessStartInfo {
                FileName - "python",
                Arguments = $"image_predict.py
\"{imagePath}\"",
                RedirectStandardOutput = true,
                UseShellExecute = false,
                CreateNoWindow = true
            };
```

```
        Process          process          =
Process.Start(psi);
        process.WaitForExit();
        return
process.StandardOutput.ReadToEnd().Trim();
    }
  }
}
```

Running the C# Image Recognition App

Train the image classifier:

```sh

python train_model.py
```

Run the C# app, select an image, and click "Predict". Output Example:

```makefile

Prediction: Labrador Retriever
```

191

Conclusion

In this chapter, we:
Trained a **machine learning model in Python**
Integrated ML into a **C# WPF app**
Built an **image recognition system** using **Python and C#**

Next, we will explore **"Cloud Deployment and Serverless Applications"**.

Shall we proceed with **Chapter 15: Cloud Deployment and Serverless Applications**?

CHAPTER 15

CLOUD DEPLOYMENT AND SERVERLESS APPLICATIONS

Cloud computing enables **scalability, reliability, and cost-efficiency** by allowing applications to be hosted remotely. This chapter covers:
Hosting Python and C# apps on AWS, Azure, and Google Cloud
Deploying serverless functions with AWS Lambda (Python) and Azure Functions (C#)
A real-world example: A serverless chatbot API

1. Hosting Python and C# Apps on AWS, Azure, and Google Cloud

Hosting a Python Web App on AWS Elastic Beanstalk

AWS **Elastic Beanstalk** simplifies deploying and managing Python web applications.

Step 1: Install AWS CLI and EB CLI

sh

```
pip install awsebcli --upgrade
aws configure  # Set AWS credentials
```

Step 2: Create a Flask App (app.py)

python

```python
from flask import Flask

app = Flask(__name__)

@app.route("/")
def home():
    return "Hello from AWS!"

if __name__ == "__main__":
    app.run(host="0.0.0.0", port=5000)
```

Step 3: Initialize and Deploy the App

sh

```
eb init -p python-3.8 my-python-app
eb create my-python-env
```

Elastic Beanstalk will automatically handle deployment

Hosting a C# Web App on Azure App Service

Azure **App Service** makes it easy to host ASP.NET Core applications.

Step 1: Create an ASP.NET Core Web App

sh

```
dotnet new webapp -o MyAzureApp
cd MyAzureApp
```

Step 2: Deploy the App to Azure

sh

```
az login
az      webapp      create      --resource-group
MyResourceGroup --plan MyAppServicePlan --name
MyAzureApp --runtime "DOTNET:7.0"
dotnet publish -c Release -o ./publish
az  webapp  deployment  source  config-zip  --
resource-group MyResourceGroup --name MyAzureApp
--src ./publish.zip
```

Visit your deployed app at:

arduino

```
https://myazureapp.azurewebsites.net
```

Hosting a Python & C# App on Google Cloud Run

Google Cloud Run allows **serverless container hosting**.

Step 1: Containerize the App (for Python & C#)

Create a Dockerfile:

dockerfile

```
FROM python:3.8
 . /app
WORKDIR /app
RUN pip install flask
CMD ["python", "app.py"]
```

Step 2: Deploy to Cloud Run

sh

```
gcloud builds submit --tag gcr.io/my-project/my-app
gcloud run deploy my-app --image gcr.io/my-project/my-app --platform managed
```

Cloud Run automatically scales the application.

---

2. Deploying Serverless Functions with AWS Lambda (Python) and Azure Functions (C#)

AWS Lambda: Serverless Python Function

Step 1: Install AWS CLI and Set Up Lambda

sh

```
aws configure  # Set AWS credentials
```

Step 2: Write the Python Lambda Function (lambda_function.py)

python

```python
import json

def lambda_handler(event, context):
    name = event.get("name", "World")
    return {
        "statusCode": 200,
        "body": json.dumps(f"Hello, {name}!")
    }
```

Step 3: Deploy to AWS Lambda

sh

```sh
zip function.zip lambda_function.py
aws lambda create-function --function-name
HelloWorldLambda --runtime python3.8 --role
myIAMRole                        --handler
lambda_function.lambda_handler    --zip-file
fileb://function.zip
```

Invoke the Lambda function:

sh

```
aws      lambda      invoke      --function-name
HelloWorldLambda response.json
```

Response:

```
json
```

```
{"statusCode": 200, "body": "Hello, World!"}
```

Azure Functions: Serverless C# Function

Step 1: Install Azure CLI and Create a Function
```sh
sh
```

```sh
az login
az    functionapp    create    --resource-group
MyResourceGroup    --consumption-plan-location
westeurope --runtime dotnet --name MyFunctionApp
```

Step 2: Write the C# Function (Function.cs)
```csharp
csharp
```

```csharp
using System.IO;
using Microsoft.AspNetCore.Mvc;
using Microsoft.Azure.WebJobs;
using Microsoft.AspNetCore.Http;
using Newtonsoft.Json;
```

```
public static class HelloFunction {
    [FunctionName("HelloFunction")]
    public static IActionResult Run(
        [HttpTrigger("GET", "POST")] HttpRequest
req) {

        string name = req.Query["name"];
        return new OkObjectResult($"Hello, {name
?? "World"}!");
    }
}
```

Step 3: Deploy to Azure Functions

```sh
func azure functionapp publish MyFunctionApp
```

Invoke via HTTP Request:

```arduino
https://myfunctionapp.azurewebsites.net/api/Hel
loFunction?name=Alice
```

Response:

```json
"Hello, Alice!"
```

3. Real-World Example: A Serverless Chatbot API

Now, let's build a **serverless chatbot** using AWS Lambda (Python) and Azure Functions (C#).

Step 1: Write the Chatbot Logic in Python

Create `chatbot.py`:

```python
import json

responses = {
    "hello": "Hi there!",
    "how are you": "I'm doing great, thanks!",
    "bye": "Goodbye!"
}

def chatbot(message):
    return  responses.get(message.lower(),  "I
don't understand.")

def lambda_handler(event, context):
    user_message = event.get("message", "")
    response = chatbot(user_message)
    return {
```

```
"statusCode": 200,
"body": json.dumps(response)
}
```

Step 2: Deploy to AWS Lambda

sh

```
zip chatbot.zip chatbot.py
aws lambda create-function --function-name
ChatbotLambda --runtime python3.8 --role
myIAMRole --handler chatbot.lambda_handler --
zip-file fileb://chatbot.zip
```

Invoke the chatbot function:

sh

```
aws lambda invoke --function-name ChatbotLambda
--payload '{"message": "hello"}' response.json
```

Response:

json

```
{"statusCode": 200, "body": "Hi there!"}
```

Step 3: Deploy the Chatbot on Azure Functions (C#)

Modify `Function.cs`:

csharp

```csharp
using System;
using Microsoft.AspNetCore.Mvc;
using Microsoft.Azure.WebJobs;
using Microsoft.AspNetCore.Http;
using Newtonsoft.Json;
using System.Threading.Tasks;

public static class ChatbotFunction {
    [FunctionName("ChatbotFunction")]
    public static async Task<IActionResult> Run(
        [HttpTrigger("POST")] HttpRequest req) {

        string requestBody = await new
StreamReader(req.Body).ReadToEndAsync();
        dynamic data =
JsonConvert.DeserializeObject(requestBody);
        string message =
data?.message?.ToLower();

        var responses = new Dictionary<string,
string> {
            {"hello", "Hi there!"},
```

```
        {"how  are  you",  "I'm  doing  great,
thanks!"},
        {"bye", "Goodbye!"}
    };

    string          reply          =
responses.ContainsKey(message)               ?
responses[message] : "I don't understand.";
    return new OkObjectResult(reply);
  }
}
```

Deploy to Azure Functions

sh

```
func azure functionapp publish MyChatbotApp
```

Test with HTTP Request:

sh

```
curl              -X              POST
https://mychatbotapp.azurewebsites.net/api/Chat
botFunction -H "Content-Type: application/json"
-d '{"message": "hello"}'
```

Response:

json

```
"Hi there!"
```

Conclusion

In   this   chapter,   we:

Deployed Python & C# apps on AWS, Azure, and Google   Cloud

Created serverless functions with AWS Lambda & Azure   Functions

Built a real-world chatbot API using cloud functions

Next, we'll explore **"Cybersecurity and Secure Coding Practices"** to protect applications against threats.

Shall we proceed with **Chapter 16: Cybersecurity and Secure Coding Practices**?

PART 5

SECURITY, TESTING, AND DEPLOYMENT

CHAPTER 16

SECURITY BEST PRACTICES FOR CROSS-PLATFORM APPLICATIONS

Security is paramount in application development, especially for **cross-platform applications**. As applications span multiple environments (Windows, macOS, Linux, mobile), ensuring that they are **secure, robust, and resilient** is critical. This chapter covers: **Handling authentication and authorization Secure coding practices in Python and C# Encryption and hashing techniques A real-world example: A secure password manager**

---

1. Handling Authentication and Authorization

Authentication vs. Authorization

- **Authentication**: Verifying the identity of a user (e.g., through a username/password).

- **Authorization**: Determining what resources a user can access once authenticated (e.g., permissions).

Authentication Best Practices

- Use **multi-factor authentication (MFA)** to add an extra layer of security.
- Avoid storing **plain-text passwords**. Use **hashing** for storing passwords securely.
- Use **OAuth2** or **JWT (JSON Web Tokens)** for managing user sessions.

Python: Implementing Basic Authentication with Flask

Let's create a simple **login system** with **JWT authentication** using Python.

Install dependencies:

```sh
sh
```

```
pip install flask pyjwt
```

app.py - Flask API with JWT Authentication

```python
python
```

```python
from flask import Flask, request, jsonify
import jwt
import datetime

app = Flask(__name__)
app.config["SECRET_KEY"] = "mysecretkey"

# Fake user for demonstration
user = {"username": "alice", "password":
"password123"}

@app.route("/login", methods=["POST"])
def login():
    auth = request.json
    if auth["username"] == user["username"] and
auth["password"] == user["password"]:
        # Create JWT token
        token = jwt.encode({"user":
auth["username"], "exp":
datetime.datetime.utcnow() +
datetime.timedelta(hours=1)},
app.config["SECRET_KEY"], algorithm="HS256")
        return jsonify({"token": token})
    return jsonify({"message": "Invalid
credentials"}), 401

@app.route("/protected", methods=["GET"])
def protected():
    token = request.headers.get("Authorization")
```

```python
    if not token:
        return jsonify({"message": "Token is
missing!"}), 403
    try:
        token = token.split(" ")[1]
        decoded        =        jwt.decode(token,
app.config["SECRET_KEY"], algorithms=["HS256"])
        return jsonify({"message": f"Hello
{decoded['user']}!"})
    except jwt.ExpiredSignatureError:
        return jsonify({"message": "Token has
expired!"}), 401
    except jwt.InvalidTokenError:
        return jsonify({"message": "Invalid
token!"}), 403

if __name__ == "__main__":
    app.run(debug=True)
```

How it works:

Login: Accepts a POST request, checks credentials, and generates a **JWT** **token**. **Protected route**: Requires the **JWT token** to access the protected resource.

C#: JWT Authentication with ASP.NET Core

Step 1: Install NuGet Packages

sh

```sh
dotnet                    add                  package
Microsoft.AspNetCore.Authentication.JwtBearer
```

Step 2: Configure JWT in `Startup.cs`

csharp

```csharp
public void ConfigureServices(IServiceCollection
services) {

services.AddAuthentication(JwtBearerDefaults.Au
thenticationScheme)
            .AddJwtBearer(options => {
                options.RequireHttpsMetadata   =
false;

options.TokenValidationParameters     =     new
TokenValidationParameters {
                    ValidateIssuer = false,
                    ValidateAudience = false,
                    ValidateLifetime = true,
                    IssuerSigningKey    =    new
SymmetricSecurityKey(Encoding.UTF8.GetBytes("my
secretkey"))
                };
            });
    services.AddControllers();
}
```

```csharp
public void Configure(IApplicationBuilder app,
IWebHostEnvironment env) {
    app.UseAuthentication();
    app.UseAuthorization();
    app.UseEndpoints(endpoints => {
        endpoints.MapControllers();
    });
}
```

Step 3: Create a Controller with JWT Authentication

csharp

```csharp
[Route("api/[controller]")]
[ApiController]
public class AuthController : ControllerBase {
    [HttpPost("login")]
    public IActionResult Login([FromBody]
LoginRequest request) {
        if (request.Username == "alice" &&
request.Password == "password123") {
            var claims = new[] {
                new Claim(ClaimTypes.Name,
request.Username)
            };
            var key = new
SymmetricSecurityKey(Encoding.UTF8.GetBytes("my
secretkey"));
```

211

```
            var        creds       =        new
SigningCredentials(key,
SecurityAlgorithms.HmacSha256);
        var token = new JwtSecurityToken(
            expires:
DateTime.Now.AddHours(1),
            signingCredentials: creds,
            claims: claims
        );
        return   Ok(new   {   Token   =   new
JwtSecurityTokenHandler().WriteToken(token) });
    }
    return Unauthorized();
  }


  [Authorize]
  [HttpGet("protected")]
  public IActionResult Protected() {
      return Ok("Hello, authenticated user!");
  }
}
```

How   it   works:

Login: Returns a JWT token when valid credentials are provided.

Protected: Requires a valid JWT token to access.

2. Secure Coding Practices in Python and C#

Python Secure Coding Best Practices

- **Validate user input**: Always validate input to avoid **SQL injection** and other attacks.
- **Use HTTPS**: Always use **SSL/TLS encryption** for data transmission.
- **Use environment variables** for storing sensitive information like API keys, passwords, and secret keys.

Example: Using Environment Variables in Python

```python
python

import os
from dotenv import load_dotenv

load_dotenv()  # Load environment variables from
.env file
secret_key = os.getenv("SECRET_KEY")
print(secret_key)
```

C# Secure Coding Best Practices

- **Use parameterized queries** to avoid SQL injection.
- **Avoid hardcoding sensitive information** (e.g., database connection strings) in your source code.

213

- **Sanitize user input** and **validate** to prevent **XSS (cross-site scripting)**.

Example: Using Environment Variables in C#

csharp

```
var                    secretKey                    =
Environment.GetEnvironmentVariable("SECRET_KEY"
);
Console.WriteLine(secretKey);
```

3. Encryption and Hashing

Encryption

Encryption is used to **secure data** by converting it into unreadable text that can only be decrypted with a key.

Python: AES Encryption with `pycryptodome`

sh

```
pip install pycryptodome
python
```

```
from Crypto.Cipher import AES
from Crypto.Util.Padding import pad, unpad
from Crypto.Random import get_random_bytes
```

214

```
# Key and data
key = get_random_bytes(16)
data = b"Sensitive Data"

# Encryption
cipher = AES.new(key, AES.MODE_CBC)
ciphertext      =      cipher.encrypt(pad(data,
AES.block_size))

# Decryption
decipher    =    AES.new(key,    AES.MODE_CBC,
iv=cipher.iv)
plaintext = unpad(decipher.decrypt(ciphertext),
AES.block_size)

print(plaintext.decode())
```

Hashing

Hashing is used for **one-way encryption** where the original data cannot be recovered.

Python: Hashing with bcrypt

```sh
```

```
pip install bcrypt
python
```

```
import bcrypt

# Hashing a password
password = b"password123"
hashed            =              bcrypt.hashpw(password,
bcrypt.gensalt())

# Verifying the password
if bcrypt.checkpw(password, hashed):
    print("Password match")
else:
    print("Password does not match")
```

C#: Hashing with SHA256

```
csharp

using System;
using System.Security.Cryptography;
using System.Text;

public class Program {
    public static void Main() {
        string password = "password123";
        using      (SHA256      sha256Hash      =
SHA256.Create()) {
```

```
        byte[]          bytes          =
sha256Hash.ComputeHash(Encoding.UTF8.GetBytes(p
assword));
        StringBuilder   builder   =   new
StringBuilder();
        foreach (byte b in bytes) {

builder.Append(b.ToString("x2"));
        }
        Console.WriteLine($"Hash:
{builder.ToString()}");
    }
  }
}
```

4. Real-World Example: A Secure Password Manager

A **secure password manager** stores and manages user credentials with **encryption**.

Step 1: Python Secure Password Manager
```
python
```

```python
import bcrypt
import json
from Crypto.Cipher import AES
from Crypto.Util.Padding import pad, unpad
from Crypto.Random import get_random_bytes
```

```
# Encrypt the password before saving
def encrypt_password(password, key):
    cipher = AES.new(key, AES.MODE_CBC)
    ciphertext                          =
cipher.encrypt(pad(password.encode(),
AES.block_size))
    return cipher.iv + ciphertext


# Save password securely
def save_password(username, password):
    key = get_random_bytes(16)
    encrypted = encrypt_password(password, key)
    with open(f"{username}_password.json", "wb")
as f:
        f.write(encrypted)


# Load password securely
def load_password(username):
    with open(f"{username}_password.json", "rb")
as f:
        data = f.read()
    key = get_random_bytes(16)   # Normally, you
would retrieve this from a secure place
    iv = data[:16]
    ciphertext = data[16:]
    cipher = AES.new(key, AES.MODE_CBC, iv=iv)
```

```
    plaintext                        =
unpad(cipher.decrypt(ciphertext),
AES.block_size)
    return plaintext.decode()

# Example usage
save_password("alice", "mySecureP@ssw0rd!")
print(load_password("alice"))
```

Step 2: C# Secure Password Manager

csharp

```
using System;
using System.IO;
using System.Security.Cryptography;
using System.Text;

class PasswordManager {
    public  static  void  SavePassword(string
username, string password) {
        using (Aes aesAlg = Aes.Create()) {
            aesAlg.Key                   =
Encoding.UTF8.GetBytes("my16ByteSecretKey");
            aesAlg.IV  =  new  byte[16];  //
Initialization vector

            ICryptoTransform  encryptor  =
aesAlg.CreateEncryptor(aesAlg.Key, aesAlg.IV);
```

```
            using (MemoryStream msEncrypt = new
MemoryStream()) {
                using (CryptoStream csEncrypt =
new       CryptoStream(msEncrypt,        encryptor,
CryptoStreamMode.Write)) {
                    using              (StreamWriter
swEncrypt = new StreamWriter(csEncrypt)) {

swEncrypt.Write(password);
                    }
                }

File.WriteAllBytes($"{username}_password.txt",
msEncrypt.ToArray());
            }
        }
    }


    public  static  string  LoadPassword(string
username) {
        byte[]            cipherText            =
File.ReadAllBytes($"{username}_password.txt");

        using (Aes aesAlg = Aes.Create()) {
            aesAlg.Key                           =
Encoding.UTF8.GetBytes("my16ByteSecretKey");
            aesAlg.IV = new byte[16];
```

```csharp
            ICryptoTransform    decryptor    =
aesAlg.CreateDecryptor(aesAlg.Key, aesAlg.IV);
            using (MemoryStream msDecrypt = new
MemoryStream(cipherText)) {
                using (CryptoStream csDecrypt =
new     CryptoStream(msDecrypt,       decryptor,
CryptoStreamMode.Read)) {
                    using (StreamReader reader =
new StreamReader(csDecrypt)) {
                        return
reader.ReadToEnd();
                    }
                }
            }
        }
    }

    static void Main() {
        SavePassword("alice",
"mySecureP@ssw0rd!");

Console.WriteLine(LoadPassword("alice"));
    }
}
```

221

Conclusion

In this chapter, we:

Handled authentication and authorization with **JWT**

Implemented secure coding practices in Python and C#

Used encryption and hashing to secure data

Built a secure password manager using encryption

Next, we'll dive into **"Automated Testing and Continuous Integration"** to ensure that your applications are robust and scalable.

Shall we proceed with **Chapter 17: Automated Testing and Continuous Integration**?

CHAPTER 17

AUTOMATED TESTING AND DEBUGGING

Automated testing ensures that your application works as expected and reduces the risk of introducing bugs during development. Debugging is equally important for identifying and fixing issues in your code efficiently. This chapter   covers:

Unit testing with PyTest (Python) and xUnit (C#)
Debugging techniques in Visual Studio and VS Code
A real-world example: Automating tests for a web API

---

1. Unit Testing with PyTest (Python) and xUnit (C#)

Unit Testing with PyTest (Python)

PyTest is a popular testing framework for Python that makes it easy to write simple as well as scalable test cases.

Step 1: Install PyTest

sh

```
pip install pytest
```

Step 2: Write a Simple Python Function

Let's write a function to calculate the **square of a number**.

```
python
```

```python
def square(number):
    return number * number
```

Step 3: Write Unit Tests Using PyTest

Create a `test_example.py` file.

```
python
```

```python
import pytest
from example import square

def test_square_positive():
    assert square(3) == 9

def test_square_negative():
    assert square(-4) == 16

def test_square_zero():
    assert square(0) == 0
```

Step 4: Run PyTest

```
sh
```

```
pytest
```

PyTest will automatically discover and run the tests, providing a **detailed report** on which tests passed or failed.

Unit Testing with xUnit (C#)

xUnit is a widely-used testing framework for **.NET** applications.

Step 1: Install xUnit

You can install xUnit via NuGet or directly from the **.NET CLI**.

```sh
sh
```

```
dotnet add package xunit
dotnet add package xunit.runner.visualstudio
```
Step 2: Write a Simple C# Function

Let's write a function that calculates the **square of a number** in C#.

```csharp
csharp
```

```
public class MathOperations {
    public int Square(int number) {
        return number * number;
    }
}
```

Step 3: Write Unit Tests Using xUnit

Create a test file MathOperationsTests.cs.

csharp

using Xunit;

```
public class MathOperationsTests {
    private        readonly        MathOperations
_mathOperations = new MathOperations();

    [Fact]
    public void Test_Square_Positive() {
        Assert.Equal(9,
_mathOperations.Square(3));
    }

    [Fact]
    public void Test_Square_Negative() {
        Assert.Equal(16,
_mathOperations.Square(-4));
    }
```

```
    [Fact]
    public void Test_Square_Zero() {
        Assert.Equal(0,
_mathOperations.Square(0));
    }
}
```

Step 4: Run the Tests

```sh
```

```
dotnet test
```

xUnit will execute the tests and provide a test report indicating which tests passed or failed.

2. Debugging Techniques in Visual Studio and VS Code

Debugging in Visual Studio (C#)

Visual Studio provides a comprehensive debugging environment for C# development, offering features like breakpoints, variable watches, and call stacks.

Step 1: Set a Breakpoint

- **Set a breakpoint** by clicking on the **left margin** next to the line of code where you want the execution to pause.

Step 2: Start Debugging

- Press **F5** to **start debugging** or click on the **Start Debugging** button in the toolbar. The program will run and pause at your breakpoints.

Step 3: Inspect Variables

- Once paused at a breakpoint, you can inspect **variables**, step through the code (F10 for Step Over, F11 for Step Into), and view the **Call Stack**.

Step 4: Conditional Breakpoints

- Right-click on a breakpoint and choose **Conditions** to set breakpoints that only trigger when a specific condition is met (e.g., when a variable equals a certain value).

Debugging in Visual Studio Code (Python)

Visual Studio Code (VS Code) provides lightweight debugging tools for Python using the **Python extension**.

Step 1: Install Python Extension

Install the **Python extension** for VS Code if you haven't already.

Step 2: Set a Breakpoint

Click in the **gutter** next to the line number where you want to set a breakpoint.

Step 3: Configure Debugging

Create a `.vscode/launch.json` configuration file to define how your app is run and debugged. VS Code often creates this automatically for Python apps.

Step 4: Start Debugging

Press **F5** or go to the **Run and Debug** view in the sidebar and click **Start Debugging**. The program will pause at the breakpoints, allowing you to inspect variables and step through the code.

Step 5: Watch Expressions

In the **Debug** pane, you can **watch expressions** to monitor the values of variables during debugging.

---

3. Real-World Example: Automating Tests for a Web API

We will now create a **simple Flask web API** and automate its testing using **PyTest** (Python) and **xUnit** (C#).

Step 1: Build a Flask Web API

Create a simple Flask API (`app.py`) that manages **user data**.

```python
from flask import Flask, jsonify

app = Flask(__name__)

users = [
    {"id": 1, "name": "Alice"},
    {"id": 2, "name": "Bob"}
]
```

230

```
@app.route("/users", methods=["GET"])
def get_users():
    return jsonify(users)


@app.route("/users/<int:id>", methods=["GET"])
def get_user(id):
    user = next((u for u in users if u["id"] ==
id), None)
    return jsonify(user) if user else ("Not
found", 404)


if __name__ == "__main__":
    app.run(debug=True)
```

Step 2: Write PyTest Tests for the API

Create a test_app.py file with the following tests using PyTest:

python

```
import pytest
from app import app


@pytest.fixture
def client():
    with app.test_client() as client:
        yield client
```

231

```python
def test_get_users(client):
    response = client.get("/users")
    assert response.status_code == 200
    assert len(response.json) == 2

def test_get_user(client):
    response = client.get("/users/1")
    assert response.status_code == 200
    assert response.json["name"] == "Alice"

def test_get_user_not_found(client):
    response = client.get("/users/999")
    assert response.status_code == 404
```

Step 3: Run the Tests

```sh
sh
```

```
pytest
```

PyTest will run the tests, and you'll see the results in the terminal.

Step 4: Write xUnit Tests for the API (C#)

Create a C# **API Client** (`ApiClient.cs`) that interacts with the Flask API. Then, write unit tests using **xUnit**.

```csharp
csharp

using System.Net.Http;
using System.Threading.Tasks;
using Newtonsoft.Json;
using Xunit;

public class ApiClient {
    private readonly HttpClient _client;

    public ApiClient() {
        _client = new HttpClient();
    }

    public async Task<string> GetUser(int id) {
        var response = await
_client.GetStringAsync($"http://127.0.0.1:5000/
users/{id}");
        return response;
    }
}

public class ApiClientTests {
    private readonly ApiClient _client = new
ApiClient();
```

233

```
[Fact]
public async Task Test_GetUser_ValidId() {
    var response = await _client.GetUser(1);
    var                     user                  =
JsonConvert.DeserializeObject<dynamic>(response
);
    Assert.Equal("Alice",
user.name.ToString());
    }


[Fact]
public async Task Test_GetUser_InvalidId() {
    await
Assert.ThrowsAsync<HttpRequestException>(()   =>
_client.GetUser(999));
    }
}
```

Conclusion

In   this   chapter,   we:
Set up unit tests with **PyTest (Python)** and **xUnit (C#)**
Learned debugging techniques in **Visual Studio** and **VS Code**
Automated tests for a web API using both Python and C#

Next, we'll dive into **"Continuous Integration and Deployment (CI/CD)"** to ensure smooth deployment pipelines and automated releases.

Shall we proceed with **Chapter 18: Continuous Integration and Deployment (CI/CD)**?

CHAPTER 18

PACKAGING AND DEPLOYMENT STRATEGIES

Effective deployment strategies ensure that your applications are easy to distribute, scale, and maintain. In this chapter, we'll explore: **Creating executables for Windows, macOS, and Linux Dockerizing Python and C# applications A real-world example: Deploying a Flask and .NET API with Docker**

---

1. Creating Executables for Windows, macOS, and Linux

Creating Executables for Python

Python is typically run in an interpreter, but you can **package Python applications into standalone executables** using tools like **PyInstaller**.

Step 1: Install PyInstaller

sh

```
pip install pyinstaller
```

Step 2: Create a Simple Python Script

Let's say you have a Python script `app.py` that you want to package.

```
python
```

```
# app.py
print("Hello, World!")
```

Step 3: Create the Executable

Run the following command in the terminal to create an executable:

```
sh
```

```
pyinstaller --onefile app.py
```

This will generate an executable in the `dist` folder.

- **For Windows**, it will create a `.exe` file.
- **For macOS**, it will create a `.app` bundle.
- **For Linux**, it will generate a standalone binary.

You can now distribute the executable for the respective OS. No need for users to have Python installed.

Creating Executables for C# (.NET Core)

C# applications can be packaged as **self-contained** executables using the **.NET CLI**.

Step 1: Create a Simple C# Application

Create a simple application (`Program.cs`):

```csharp
using System;

class Program {
    static void Main() {
        Console.WriteLine("Hello, World!");
    }
}
```

Step 2: Publish the Executable

To create a standalone executable for **Windows**, **macOS**, or **Linux**, run the following command:

```sh
dotnet publish -c Release -r win-x64 --self-contained true
```

For **macOS** or **Linux**, change the `-r` flag accordingly:

- `win-x64` for Windows
- `osx-x64` for macOS
- `linux-x64` for Linux

Step 3: Distribute the Executable

Once published, you can distribute the `.exe`, `.app`, or binary for the corresponding platform.

2. Dockerizing Python and C# Applications

Docker is a powerful tool for packaging applications into containers that can run consistently across different environments.

Dockerizing a Python Application

Step 1: Create a Simple Python Application

Create a simple Flask app (`app.py`):

```python
from flask import Flask

app = Flask(__name__)

@app.route("/")
def home():
    return "Hello, Dockerized World!"

if __name__ == "__main__":
    app.run(debug=True, host="0.0.0.0")
```

Step 2: Create a Dockerfile for Python

Create a `Dockerfile` in the same directory as your Python app:

```dockerfile
# Use the official Python image from Docker Hub
FROM python:3.9-slim

# Set the working directory in the container
```

```
WORKDIR /app

# the current directory contents into the
container at /app
 . /app

# Install dependencies
RUN pip install --no-cache-dir -r
requirements.txt

# Expose the port the app runs on
EXPOSE 5000

# Run the application
CMD ["python", "app.py"]
```

Step 3: Build and Run the Docker Container

Build the image:

```sh
docker build -t my-python-app .
```

Run the container:

```sh
docker run -p 5000:5000 my-python-app
```

Step 4: Access the Application

Visit the Flask app at `http://localhost:5000`. Your Python application is now **Dockerized**.

Dockerizing a C# Application

Step 1: Create a Simple C# API

Create a basic **ASP.NET Core API** (`Program.cs`):

```csharp
using Microsoft.AspNetCore.Builder;
using Microsoft.AspNetCore.Hosting;
using Microsoft.Extensions.Hosting;

var builder = WebApplication.CreateBuilder(args);
var app = builder.Build();

app.MapGet("/", () => "Hello, Dockerized World!");

app.Run();
```

Step 2: Create a Dockerfile for C#

Create a `Dockerfile` in the root directory:

```dockerfile
dockerfile

# Use the official .NET SDK image to build the
app
FROM mcr.microsoft.com/dotnet/aspnet:6.0 AS base
WORKDIR /app
EXPOSE 80

# Use the official .NET SDK image to build and
publish the app
FROM mcr.microsoft.com/dotnet/sdk:6.0 AS build
WORKDIR /src
 ["MyApp/MyApp.csproj", "MyApp/"]
RUN dotnet restore "MyApp/MyApp.csproj"
 . .
WORKDIR "/src/MyApp"
RUN dotnet build "MyApp.csproj" -c Release -o
/app/build
RUN dotnet publish "MyApp.csproj" -c Release -o
/app/publish

#  the build to the base image and set entry point
FROM base AS final
WORKDIR /app
 --from=build /app/publish .
```

```
ENTRYPOINT ["dotnet", "MyApp.dll"]
```

Step 3: Build and Run the Docker Container

Build the Docker image:

```sh
sh
```

```
docker build -t my-dotnet-app .
```

Run the container:

```sh
sh
```

```
docker run -p 8080:80 my-dotnet-app
```

Step 4: Access the Application

Visit the C# API at `http://localhost:8080`. Your **C# application is now Dockerized**.

---

3. Real-World Example: Deploying a Flask and .NET API with Docker

We'll now deploy a **Flask API** and a **.NET API** together using Docker and Docker Compose.

Step 1: Directory Structure

```bash
/my-app
  /flask-api
    /Dockerfile
    /app.py
    /requirements.txt
  /dotnet-api
    /Dockerfile
    /Program.cs
```

Step 2: Docker Compose Configuration

Create a `docker-compose.yml` file to manage both applications:

```yaml
version: '3.4'

services:
  flask-api:
    build: ./flask-api
    ports:
      - "5000:5000"
  dotnet-api:
    build: ./dotnet-api
    ports:
      - "8080:80"
```

Step 3: Build and Run the Docker Containers

Run Docker Compose to build and start both services:

sh

```
docker-compose up --build
```
Step 4: Access the APIs

- **Flask API**: http://localhost:5000
- **.NET API**: http://localhost:8080

Both APIs are now **running side by side** in isolated containers.

Conclusion

In this chapter, we:
Created executables for **Python and C#** for cross-platform deployment
Dockerized Python and C# applications for consistent, isolated environments
Deployed a Flask and .NET API using **Docker Compose** for a multi-container setup

Next, we will dive into **"Monitoring, Logging, and Maintenance"** to keep applications healthy and performant in production.

Shall we proceed with **Chapter 19: Monitoring, Logging, and Maintenance**?

CHAPTER 19

PERFORMANCE OPTIMIZATION AND SCALING

Optimizing the performance of your application is crucial, especially when scaling to handle **increased traffic** or **complex computations**. This chapter covers: **Profiling and optimizing Python and C# code Caching strategies and memory management Real-world example: Optimizing a high-traffic API**

1. Profiling and Optimizing Python and C# Code

Profiling and Optimizing Python Code

Profiling is the process of identifying performance bottlenecks in your code. Python provides several tools to help profile and optimize performance.

Step 1: Profiling Python Code Using `cProfile`

`cProfile` is a built-in Python module that provides detailed performance statistics for your code.

python

```python
import cProfile

def slow_function():
    total = 0
    for i in range(1000000):
        total += i
    return total


# Profile the slow function
cProfile.run('slow_function()')
```

Output:

sh

```
         4 function calls in 0.123 seconds

   Ordered by: standard name

   ncalls   tottime   percall   cumtime   percall
filename:lineno(function)
        1     0.123     0.123     0.123     0.123
slow_function.py:4(slow_function)
```

249

```
       1     0.000     0.000     0.123     0.123
<string>:1(<module>)
       1     0.000     0.000     0.123     0.123
{built-in method builtins.exec}
       1     0.000     0.000     0.000     0.000
{method 'disable' of '_lsprof.Profiler' objects}
```

Step 2: Optimizing Code Using `timeit`

For small code snippets, `timeit` can help measure the execution time.

```python
import timeit

# Measure time for a loop
print(timeit.timeit("sum(range(1000000))",
number=100))
```

Step 3: Use Built-In Python Functions

- Avoid unnecessary loops. Python's built-in functions (like `sum()`, `map()`, `filter()`, etc.) are often **optimized** and faster than loops.

Example of optimization:

```python
```

```
# Instead of using a loop, use a list
comprehension
total = sum(i for i in range(1000000))  # Faster
than using a loop
```

Profiling and Optimizing C# Code

C# also provides profiling tools to monitor performance.

Step 1: Profiling C# Code Using Visual Studio Diagnostic Tools

Visual Studio comes with **built-in diagnostic tools** to help identify performance bottlenecks in your C# application.

1. **Start debugging** your application in Visual Studio.
2. Go to **Debug** > **Windows** > **Diagnostic Tools**.
3. Monitor metrics like **CPU usage**, **memory**, and **network usage** in real-time.
4. Set breakpoints and inspect code to identify bottlenecks.

Step 2: Use Stopwatch to Measure Performance

```
csharp

using System;
using System.Diagnostics;

class Program {
```

```
static void Main() {
    Stopwatch stopwatch = new Stopwatch();
    stopwatch.Start();

    // Code to measure
    int total = 0;
    for (int i = 0; i < 1000000; i++) {
        total += i;
    }

    stopwatch.Stop();
    Console.WriteLine($"Execution        Time:
{stopwatch.ElapsedMilliseconds} ms");
    }
}
```

Step 3: Optimize C# Code

- **Avoid unnecessary allocations**. Reuse objects and collections where possible.
- **Use value types** (like `int`, `struct`) instead of reference types to reduce memory overhead.
- **Leverage parallelism** for computationally intensive tasks using **`Parallel.For`** or **`async/await`**.

2. Caching Strategies and Memory Management

Caching Strategies

Caching is used to store frequently accessed data in memory for fast retrieval.

Step 1: In-Memory Caching in Python

Python's **functools.lru_cache** decorator is an easy way to cache the results of functions.

```python
from functools import lru_cache

@lru_cache(maxsize=100)
def expensive_function(n):
    print(f"Calculating {n}...")
    return n * 2

# Function calls with caching
print(expensive_function(5))    # First time, calculates
print(expensive_function(5))  # Second time, uses cache
```

Step 2: In-Memory Caching in C#

In C#, you can use **MemoryCache** for in-memory caching.

```csharp
using System;
```

```csharp
using System.Runtime.Caching;

class Program {
    static void Main() {
        MemoryCache cache = MemoryCache.Default;

        string cacheKey = "key";
        string value = "cached value";

        // Set cache
        cache.Set(cacheKey,      value,      new
CacheItemPolicy());

        // Get cache
        string            cachedValue            =
(string)cache.Get(cacheKey);
        Console.WriteLine($"Cached      value:
{cachedValue}");
    }
}
```

Step 3: Distributed Caching for Scalability

When scaling applications across multiple instances, use **distributed caching** systems like **Redis** or **Memcached**. Both Python and C# have libraries for integrating with these systems.

- **Python Redis Example**:

```python
python

import redis

cache = redis.Redis(host='localhost', port=6379)
cache.set('key', 'value')
print(cache.get('key'))  # Output: b'value'
```

- **C# Redis Example**:

```csharp
csharp

using StackExchange.Redis;

class Program {
    static void Main() {
        ConnectionMultiplexer    redis    =
ConnectionMultiplexer.Connect("localhost");
        IDatabase db = redis.GetDatabase();
        db.StringSet("key", "value");
        Console.WriteLine(db.StringGet("key"));
    }
}
```

Memory Management

Efficient memory management ensures your application doesn't consume excessive resources, especially when scaling.

Step 1: Python Memory Management

- **Use generators** instead of lists to reduce memory usage when iterating over large datasets.

python

```
# Use a generator expression instead of a list
comprehension
gen = (x * 2 for x in range(1000000))
```

- **Use gc module** to manually collect unused memory:

python

```
import gc
gc.collect()  # Forces garbage collection
```

Step 2: C# Memory Management

- Use **Dispose()** method or **using** block to release resources like database connections, file streams, etc.

csharp

```
using (var stream = new FileStream("file.txt",
FileMode.Open)) {
    // File operations
}  // Automatically disposes the stream
```

- **Track and optimize memory usage** using **Visual Studio's Diagnostic Tools**.

---

3. Real-World Example: Optimizing a High-Traffic API

Let's consider a **high-traffic API** that needs to handle thousands of requests per second. Optimization focuses on improving performance and scalability.

Step 1: Cache Expensive Database Queries

Let's say we have an API that fetches user information from a database.

Python (Flask) Caching with Redis

python

```
import redis
from flask import Flask, jsonify

app = Flask(__name__)
cache = redis.Redis(host='localhost', port=6379)
```

```python
@app.route("/user/<int:user_id>")
def get_user(user_id):
    cached_data = cache.get(f"user:{user_id}")
    if cached_data:
        return                    jsonify({"user":
cached_data.decode()}), 200

    # Simulate a database query
    user_data = f"User {user_id} data"
    cache.set(f"user:{user_id}",        user_data,
ex=3600)   # Cache for 1 hour
    return jsonify({"user": user_data}), 200

if __name__ == "__main__":
    app.run(debug=True)
```

C# (ASP.NET Core) Caching with Redis

```
csharp
```

```csharp
public class UserController : ControllerBase {
    private readonly IDatabase _cache;

    public UserController(IConnectionMultiplexer
redis) {
        _cache = redis.GetDatabase();
    }

    [HttpGet("user/{id}")]
```

```
    public async Task<IActionResult> GetUser(int
id) {
        var         cachedUser      =          await
_cache.StringGetAsync($"user:{id}");
        if (cachedUser.HasValue) {
            return     Ok(new     {     user     =
cachedUser.ToString() });
        }

        var userData = $"User {id} data";   //
Simulate DB query
        await
_cache.StringSetAsync($"user:{id}",       userData,
TimeSpan.FromHours(1));  // Cache for 1 hour
        return Ok(new { user = userData });
    }
}
```

Step 2: Use Load Balancing and Horizontal Scaling

When traffic grows, horizontally scale your application by deploying multiple instances behind a **load balancer**. This ensures that the load is distributed evenly.

Step 3: Optimize Database Performance

- **Index frequently queried fields** in your database.
- **Use database replication** and **sharding** to scale read and write operations.

Conclusion

In this chapter, we:

Profiled and optimized Python and C# code Implemented **caching strategies** and managed **memory efficiently**

Optimized a high-traffic API by using caching and horizontal scaling

Next, we'll dive into **"Monitoring, Logging, and Maintenance"** to ensure that your application remains healthy and performant in production.

Shall we proceed with **Chapter 20: Monitoring, Logging, and Maintenance**?

CHAPTER 20

THE FUTURE OF CROSS-PLATFORM DEVELOPMENT

As we look ahead, the world of cross-platform development continues to evolve rapidly. This chapter explores the **emerging frameworks and technologies**, the growing **role of AI in application development**, and **career opportunities** in the world of Python and C# development. We will also reflect on the journey we've taken and discuss **next steps**.

1. Emerging Frameworks and Technologies

Flutter

Flutter, developed by **Google**, is gaining popularity as a **UI toolkit** for building **natively compiled applications** for mobile, web, and desktop from a single codebase. Unlike traditional cross-platform frameworks, Flutter uses **Dart** instead of JavaScript or Python.

- **Strengths**:
  - Fast development with **Hot Reload**.
  - High performance due to its **compiled nature**.
  - Wide support for **mobile, web, and desktop** apps.
- **Challenges**:
  - Smaller community compared to React Native or Xamarin.
  - Learning curve for developers unfamiliar with Dart.

.NET MAUI (Multi-platform App UI)

.NET MAUI is an evolution of Xamarin, designed to help developers create **cross-platform applications** using a single codebase in **C#**. It provides a way to develop apps for Android, iOS, macOS, and Windows.

- **Strengths**:
  - **Unified codebase** for multiple platforms.
  - Works seamlessly with **XAML** for UI design.
  - Integrates with existing **.NET tools** and **libraries**.
- **Challenges**:
  - Still evolving, with some features in preview or development.

- o Smaller developer base compared to other frameworks like Flutter or React Native.

WebAssembly (WASM)

WebAssembly (WASM) is gaining traction as a **binary instruction format** that runs in the browser. It allows applications written in **C, C++, Rust**, and even **C#** to run directly in the browser at **near-native speed**.

- **Strengths**:
  - o **Performance**: Much faster than JavaScript.
  - o Ability to run code in the **browser** without needing a plugin.
  - o Broadening language support, including **C#** and **Python**.
- **Challenges**:
  - o Limited **browser support** for certain features.
  - o Not as mature as JavaScript for full-scale app development.

Rust and Blazor

Rust is becoming an increasingly popular choice for **system-level programming** and is often used alongside **Blazor** to create fast and secure web apps. Blazor, as part of the **.NET ecosystem**, can leverage **WebAssembly** to run C# code directly in the browser.

- **Strengths**:
  - **Rust** offers high performance and memory safety.
  - **Blazor** allows for **C# code execution in the browser**, making it easier to share code across front-end and back-end.
- **Challenges**:
  - **Rust** has a steep learning curve, especially for developers used to higher-level languages.
  - **Blazor** is still evolving, and many developers prefer JavaScript frameworks for front-end development.

2. The Role of AI in Application Development

AI-Powered Tools and Frameworks

AI is no longer limited to large tech companies—**AI tools** and **frameworks** are now available to developers at all levels. Some exciting developments include:

- **AutoML (Automated Machine Learning)**: Platforms like **Google AutoML** and **Azure Machine Learning** allow developers to build machine learning models with minimal coding.
- **AI-Powered Code Completion**: Tools like **GitHub Copilot** leverage **AI** to help developers write code faster by suggesting whole lines or blocks of code based on context.
- **AI in Cross-Platform Development**: AI can optimize **UI/UX design** and **app performance** in cross-platform environments.

AI's Impact on Development

- **Automation**: AI can help **automate repetitive coding tasks**, making the development process more efficient.
- **Smarter Applications**: AI can enable applications to be more **adaptive** by analyzing user behavior and providing tailored experiences.
- **Quality Assurance**: AI-based tools can **automatically generate test cases**, detect bugs, and optimize code for performance.

AI Ethics and Development

As AI becomes more integrated into applications, it's important for developers to consider the **ethical implications** of AI, such as privacy concerns, transparency, and bias in algorithms.

3. Career Opportunities in Python and C# Development

Python Career Opportunities

Python has grown into one of the most widely-used languages, and its popularity continues to rise. Some key career opportunities for Python developers include:

- **Data Science and Machine Learning**: Python is the go-to language for data analysis, machine learning, and AI, with tools like **TensorFlow**, **PyTorch**, and **Scikit-learn**.
- **Web Development**: Python-based frameworks like **Django** and **Flask** are widely used in web development.
- **Automation**: Python is popular for automating system tasks, web scraping, and creating bots.
- **Cloud Engineering**: Python is extensively used in cloud applications and DevOps workflows, particularly with tools like **AWS Lambda** and **Google Cloud Functions**.

C# Career Opportunities

C# remains a **dominant language** in the enterprise space. Career opportunities for C# developers include:

- **Enterprise Application Development**: C# is widely used for building large-scale enterprise applications, particularly with **ASP.NET**.
- **Game Development**: **Unity**, one of the most popular game engines, uses C# for game development.
- **Cross-Platform Development**: With **Xamarin** and **.NET MAUI**, C# developers can build cross-platform mobile apps.
- **Cloud Solutions**: C# is a strong candidate for developing cloud-based solutions, particularly on **Azure**.

Full-Stack Development

Both Python and C# developers can expand into **full-stack development**, combining back-end knowledge with front-end skills. Python developers often use frameworks like **Flask** and **Django**, while C# developers can use **ASP.NET Core** combined with **JavaScript/TypeScript**.

4. Final Thoughts and Next Steps

Embrace Continuous Learning

The world of cross-platform development is **dynamic** and constantly evolving. Stay current by exploring new frameworks, tools, and techniques. Whether it's learning **new AI-driven technologies**, mastering a **new framework**, or diving deeper into **cloud computing**, the possibilities are endless.

Build Projects

There's no better way to learn than by **building real-world projects**. Experiment with the technologies and frameworks discussed in this book, and create applications that interest you. Start small and gradually scale up your projects as you gain more experience.

Contribute to Open Source

Engage with the community by contributing to open-source projects. Whether it's fixing bugs, writing documentation, or adding new features, open-source contributions can help you sharpen your skills and gain valuable experience.

Conclusion

In this chapter, we covered: **Emerging frameworks and technologies** like **Flutter**, **.NET MAUI**, and **WebAssembly**. The growing **role of AI** in application development, from **AutoML** to **AI-powered tools**. Career opportunities for **Python** and **C# developers**, ranging from **data science** to **game development**.

Cross-platform development continues to be a rapidly evolving field. Stay curious, keep building, and continue growing your skills as a developer. The future of development is full of exciting possibilities!

Thank you for following along with this book—your journey has just begun. Happy coding!

www.ingramcontent.com/pod-product-compliance
Lightning Source LLC
LaVergne TN
LVHW051439050326
832903LV00030BD/3166